# H·O·L·I·D·A·Y·S

VICTORIAN WOMEN CELEBRATE IN PENNSYLVANIA

 NADA GRAY

AN ORAL TRADITIONS PROJECT
KEYSTONE BOOKS

A Keystone Book

Published by the Pennsylvania State University Press.
215 Wagner Building, University Park, Pennsylvania
16802.

Library of Congress Cataloging in Publication Data
Gray, Nada, 1933-
Holidays: Victorian women celebrate in Pennsylvania.
Bibliography: p.
Includes index.
1. Christmas—Pennsylvania—History—19th century.
2. Easter—Pennsylvania—History—19th century.
3. Holiday decorations—Pennsylvania—History—19th
century.  I. Title

GT4986.P4G72   1983   394.2′6828′09748   83-8259
ISBN 0-271-00357-X

*Acknowledgment of the Christmas season was made with this handmade card dated 1835, 4″ h.*

## Acknowledgments

This book is about two major festivals, Christmas and Easter, but it is about much more. It is about our foremothers who nourished the holidays, cherishing and preserving the family and its traditions while adding each year something new and stylish. Although the research focuses on what was done in Pennsylvania, it is about celebrations in small towns everywhere.

It reveals what was universally fashionable in the Victorian era, a period of seventy years during which the industrial revolution affected changes in the roles of women. By the end of the first decade of the twentieth century, mass production coupled with improved transportation had made manufactured goods available everywhere while advertising had made them desirable, leaving little demand for the individual hand-crafted item. These changes in the lives of people were reflected in their celebrations—candles on the tree were snuffed out by the electric bulb, and the chicken egg shared equal billing with those of glass, metal, and celluloid. But some of this Victorian past was preserved, and hopefully this monograph, with its photographs of the old and directions for the new will allow you to accurately and sensitively re-create an earlier holiday; one which our foremothers enjoyed.

I am grateful to many people for making this book possible, the seventh in a series of Pennsylvania craft traditions produced by the Oral Traditions Project of the Union County Historical Society. A major grant was awarded to the project by the Pennsylvania Council of the Arts while the Union County Historical Society and the C. A. Reed Company of Williamsport gave additional financial assistance. Harold E. Yoder, Jr. of The Historical Society of Berks County, William T. Parsons of the Pennsylvania Folklife Society, and Dennis Moyer of the Schwenkfelder Museum provided their collections for study. In addition, Arlene Horvath and Ruth K. Hagy of Chester County Historical Society, John Aungst of Lancaster County Historical Society, Gail M. Getz and Catherine McElroy of the Pennsylvania Historical and Museum Commission, and Patricia A. Tomes and Bill Andrews of The Historical Society of York County made their collections available for photographing at the Landis Valley Farm Museum, where the director, Robert N. Sieber, provided facilities again this year. Librarians like Keith Kamm at The Atheneum; Mary Jane Stoneburg at Bucknell University; Salinda Matt at the Lancaster Historical Society; Charles Mann and Sandy Stelts at the Allison Shelley Collection, Pennsylvania State University; Roberta Bradford at the Stowe-Day Foundation; and Neville Thompson and Beatrice Taylor at Henry Francis du Pont Winterthur Museum and Library helped locate manuscripts and reference materials. In particular, collectors Thomas Anderson, the Charleses, the Cunninghams, the Elgins, the Machmers, Jim Morrison, the Kusters, Fred Neece, Malcolm Rogers, the Stableys and the Whalens shared their observations made over the years as well as their objects while researchers and writers, Jane Coleman and Phillip V. Snyder shared their information.

Then there are those whose day-to-day involvement deserves more than thanks: Joan Maurer for being willing to go to the end of the Island to see just one more ornament; Elsbeth Steffensen who cheerfully translated as well as explained German geography and history to me; Constance Timm for agreeing to work with an author whose idea of design resembles clutter and, yet, never lost her eye; Jeannette Lasansky whose ever-present enthusiasm from early morning until late at night never flagged nor found fault; and last and very personally to my husband, David, whose patience has run thin but never entirely out; my mother, Dorothy Kennedy Reichmann Kaltwasser, and grandmother, Martha Hiegelheim Kennedy, who preserved the past for me that I might leave it to my sons Brad, John, and Richard.

Nada Gray
Lewisburg, Pennsylvania
August, 1983

HRISTMAS did not become a national holiday in the United States until the 1890s when it was approved by all state legislatures. However, it was celebrated wherever there were Lutheran, Reformed, Moravian, Episcopal, or Catholic congregations. To the Puritans, which included the Methodists, Baptists, Quakers, Presbyterians and Plain people (Mennonite, Brethren, and Amish), it was just another day, and the festive antics of their neighbors were considered as popish, an anathema to those who had suffered for the Protestant Reformation. So strong was the anti-Christmas sentiment in New England that the Puritans declared the celebration illegal, imposing a fine of five shillings for anyone "found observing by abstinence from labor, feasting, or any other way, such days as Christmas day. . . ." However, the middle states of New York and Pennsylvania did not share this view. Although founded by the Quakers, Pennsylvania was also settled by Germans (Gay Dutch) of the Lutheran, Reformed, and Moravian faith who brought their traditions to this country, and the areas in which they settled are rich in folk customs concerning the two-day celebration. Alfred L. Shoemaker's *Christmas in Pennsylvania,* Earl W. Court's *4000 Years of Christmas,* and James H. Barnett's *The American Christmas* describe the customs more fully.

The acceptance of the holiday by Protestants with more puritanical backgrounds was noticeable in the literature beginning in the last half of the nineteenth century. This might be attributed in part to the efforts of Rev. Henry Harbaugh, who, in his popular publication *The Guardian,* extolled the joys of the celebration of Christmas from 1850 until his death in 1867, and who urged his fellow Protestant ministers to put these feast days back into their church calendars. That they did was evidenced by the growing popularity of the Sunday school and its Christmas presentation complete with trees, gifts, boxes of candy, and memorized recitations that were reported in the local papers: Danville Baptists had the largest tree, twenty-four feet tall, and Muncy Presbyterians sang "the sleighbell song with the accompaniment of bells and much glee." These annual Sunday school programs required a musical repertoire which did not exist, so it was provided by ministers, adding another element to the holiday. According to Maymie R. Krythe, *All About Christmas,* no carols appeared in church books before 1830 and from 1830-1860 only six were added; the majority appearing later. Among these, Henry Hopkins' (Episcopal) "We Three Kings," Phillip Brooks' "O Little Town of Bethlehem" and Edmund H. Sears' (Unitarian) "It Came Upon the Midnight Clear" are enjoyed today while others like "Gather Round the Christmas Tree" and "Carol, Brothers, Carol" have been archived with the volumes of Christmas music written, edited and published by other ministers in the last half of the nineteenth century.

In addition to religious publications, children's books, *Kriss Kringle's Book* (1842) and *Kriss Kringle's Christmas Tree* (1845), helped popularize the holiday with its jolly gift-giver and tree. Also stories appeared in women's periodicals like *Godey's Lady's Book* (1830-1891) and *Peterson's Ladies' National Magazine* (1843-1891). Both were published in Philadel-

*This 1810-1817 pencil and ink wash by John Lewis Krimmel of Philadelphia is one of the earliest drawings of a Christmas tree in Pennsylvania. It illustrates the European tradition of a table-top tree, the nascent Christmas yard, and simple decorations, $3^{13}/_{16}''$ h. Courtesy: Henry Francis du Pont Winterthur Museum, Joseph Downs Manuscript Collection, no. 59 X 5.7.*

phia and their subscription offers were advertised in all the local newspapers. Emma Wolf Bikle of Mifflinburg received a subscription for *Frank Leslie's Illustrated News* in 1884 and in that same decade Minora Meixell Kelly of Lewisburg read *Demorest's Illustrated Monthly,* presenting the latest in thought and dress from New York. About 1850 many of these magazines began hinting about the possibilities of the celebration by printing pictures of Christmas trees, stories about Christmas charity, and suggestions for making gifts and ornaments. By the 1880s, they gave directions for "planting" the tree and dressing it; by the 1890s they treated the making and giving of gifts, the adorning of the tree, and the cooking of the Christmas dinner as the accepted rule. Local newspapers like the *Mifflinburg Telegraph* in the 1880s were producing Christmas editions with carols, poems, stories, and illustrations, a departure from the apologies offered in the 1870s for not publishing the paper on Christmas day. Backed by tradition, approved by the church, and promoted by publications, Christmas entered hearts and homes throughout the country.

As Christmas entered the homes, it entered the lives of women, for during these years the home was the altar for the "cult of domesticity" where the women of the nineteenth century worshipped. One understands the period's devotion to the duty of managing a home, children, and a husband by reading the advice offered by Jennie June in *Demorest's Illustrated Monthly's* "Talks With Women" in 1865:

Work is not trouble, children are not trouble unless we make them so; husbands are very much what their wives make them; the most that we any of us require is a little more faith and a little more patience; every good thing comes in time to those who wait.

There are women who murmur at the fate that made them women at all. This is worse than useless; it is excessively stupid and silly,

*Opposite page:*

*The decoration of the church with greens, mottoes, and trees was the woman's responsibility. Many of the ornaments appear to be paper stars, crescents, and crosses. Courtesy: Union County Historical Society.*

*Identified on the back as Lutheran minister George W. Fritch with a pastor from the Union Church, this 1907 post-card presents two trees dressed for the popular Sunday school program. The cotton dressed dolls were purchased as were the honeycombed decorations which could have been produced by the Beistle Company of Shippensburg, the sole American manufacturer of meshed tissue paper for seventy-five years. Courtesy: Joe Prah, Jim Morrison.*

*Christmas is not a costly present merely, says the greater divine; it is a sentiment, a spirit, a feeling. Christmas is not an outward feast; it is within you . . .*

Harper's New Monthly Magazine, December, 1868

*The celestial gates or gates ajar appear also as a foundation for floral arrangements and a funeral tribute, but this is a tree decoration, 12" h.*

*Wreathing or roping made by stitching single leaves to a cloth background and the combination of rustic sticks and lettering were two popular Victorian wall decorations for the holidays, both at home and in the church. Courtesy: Cassell's Household Guide, Henry Francis du Pont Winterthur Museum Library: Collection of Printed Books.*

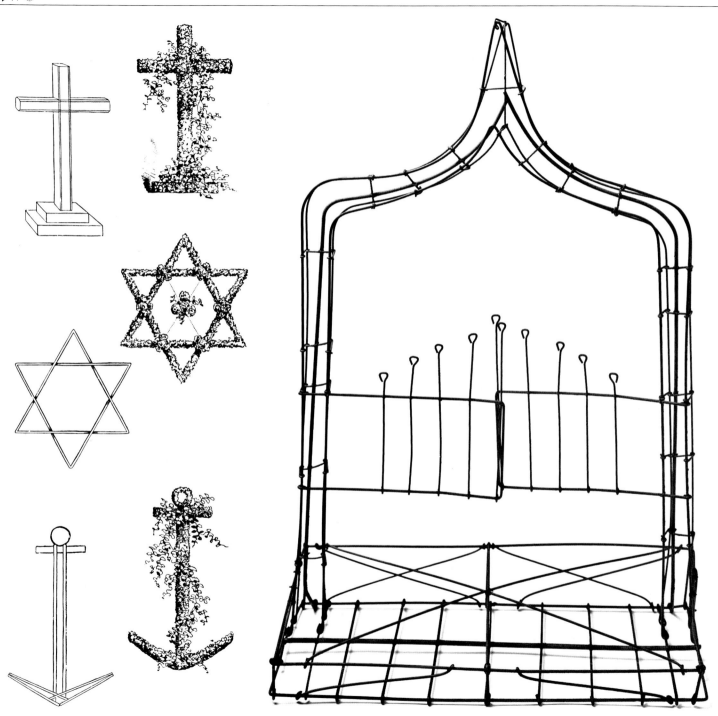

*The gas lantern or other hanging lamp in the hall needs to be well hung with bushy greenery; and in some large families where plenty of rollicking fun goes on, this is often the chosen place for a bush of mistletoe; but quiet prudent folks generally suspend the latter safely over the middle of a table or other large piece of furniture so that no one by accident or design may be able to get exactly underneath.*

Cassell's Book of the Household, Vol. II

*Directions for making forms and covering them with greens appeared in the 1888 December issue of* Ladies' Home Journal.

*Forms were available for purchase to make home and church decorations or could be ordered complete from the florist. Crosses, anchors, stars, shields, axes, and the gates ajar later became used exclusively as funeral tributes, 24" h., 15³/₄" w., 7¹/₈" d.*

*Though denounced by some editors of the women's periodicals as not suitable for Christmas, crosses were among the most popular shapes for tree dressing, 4½"-14¾"h.*

and shows plainly that they are not true women, and have never appreciated their position, its privileges, or its responsibilities.

I must confess that I am glad to be a woman, that I often pity men for being men, and never more than during the happy Christmas time or any season of holiday at home, when so much depends upon the ruling spirit of the household, and when the wife and mother enjoys the divine privilege of conferring happiness, flooding the house with interior sunshine, and unlocking such golden stores of enjoyment as were hardly known to exist.

Nor does all this require much money; it simply demands love and that inspiration of the

*Christmas is as hard on the women as an election is on the men.*

*Adamsburg Weekly Herald,* January 3, 1895

spirit which makes even the smallest item of importance that will conduce to the general good.

Let no one depreciate her office of woman, of wife, or mother. From the home, not from the world, all the best influences come; and it is woman's high privilege to guard them, to protect them, to strengthen them so that they will become hidden armor, capable of resisting the evil pressure from without, and the temptation and weakness from within.

The duties connected with this privilege are all joyful; a little onerous may be, requiring

care and judgment and forethought and patience and prayer, but very sweet, and paying most liberally for all the labor and strength invested.

For Christmas especially all one's labor should be labor of love; this is the lesson which it teaches, and the anticipations of it should be, as far as possible, unmixed with any thing but thankfulness and praise.

There is no holiday in the year which is thought of so much, or around which so many pleasant associations cling. Churches celebrate it as well as families throughout the country, and hardly a schoolhouse, even in the wilds of the distant West, but now has its annual Christmas-tree.

I said I pitied men, and I do; principally because they have neither the labor nor the pleasure of long thought and preparation. They are not trained to it; they have none of the household cares, which, while they are perplexing, are also a source of great enjoyment. They have little thought for gifts, because they put

their hands in their pockets and buy according to their means, while women eke out their small funds and render their gifts more valuable by expending them upon the work of their own hands. . . .

A very important person is the mistress of the house now, about a hundred things has she to be consulted; and in return, confidential communications are made concerning the mince-pies, the children's stockings, and the debatable question of a dressing gown or a dressing-case for papa.

If she is happy and enters with her whole heart into these preparations, how much happiness she diffuses around her; if, on the contrary, but I hope and verily believe there are few such women, she frets at and makes trouble of every thing, the atmosphere is poisoned, and Christmas is unknown though twenty turkeys were killed and the larder abounded in all the delicacies of the Christmas season. . . .

Perhaps some of my readers have never before ''kept'' Christmas, or been in the habit of thinking much of it. Let me beg them to commence now, for the sake of their families, for the sake of their children, for their own sakes, and the influence upon the world around them.

Brighten your house, open your heart, hang wreaths and branches of evergreen upon the walls. Fill your children's stockings, and have a Christmas-tree for your friends and neighbors. Shut not your door in the face of Christ, but let him see your willingness at least to acknowledge his existence and the influence of his birth, teachings, and character. . . .

Let Christmas become something more to you than a mere name, an old-fashioned observance in which you felt no interest, and took no share. Endow it with life, with the life of the heart and the soul, with the life of your affections and hopes, your efforts and your cares.

Christmas comes but once a year, but its influence remains for ever if properly appreciated and employed.

Women, armed with this advice, began to keep Christmas in the church as well as their homes. In addition to helping with the Sunday school program, women were delegated the responsibility of planning and providing, if not actually hanging, the greens in the

*Made of cotton, red glazed or flint paper, and black wool, these horses posed on the tree. Directions for making a similar fabric horse were printed in the 1888 December Godey's Lady's Book, 7¼"-11¼" h.*

*The most prominent feature of the Christmas of the present is its gift-bearing tree . . .*

Demorest's Monthly Magazine, December 1882

*We have had a busy sewing day, it is nearly Christmas. Everyone has something to do that only one or two others know anything about. Beautiful secrecy. There is a wonderful interest among all classes now in celebrating what is considered the birth time of Jesus. We used to scorn the idea of keeping Christmas when I was a child . . .*

Lavinia Yeatman's Diary/Kennett Square, December 22, 1890

*The place of honor at the top of the tree is held by a cotton-covered and tinsel-trimmed star. Other homemade and handmade ornaments include the flag, fairies, paper chains and perhaps some of the presents entwined among the branches of this twentieth-century tree. Courtesy: Jim Morrison.*

*Opposite page: Children's dreams of Santa Claus were filled with visions of stuffed animals, dolls, and the American flag in this Griffith and Griffith stereopticon view, circa 1900. Courtesy: Library of Congress.*

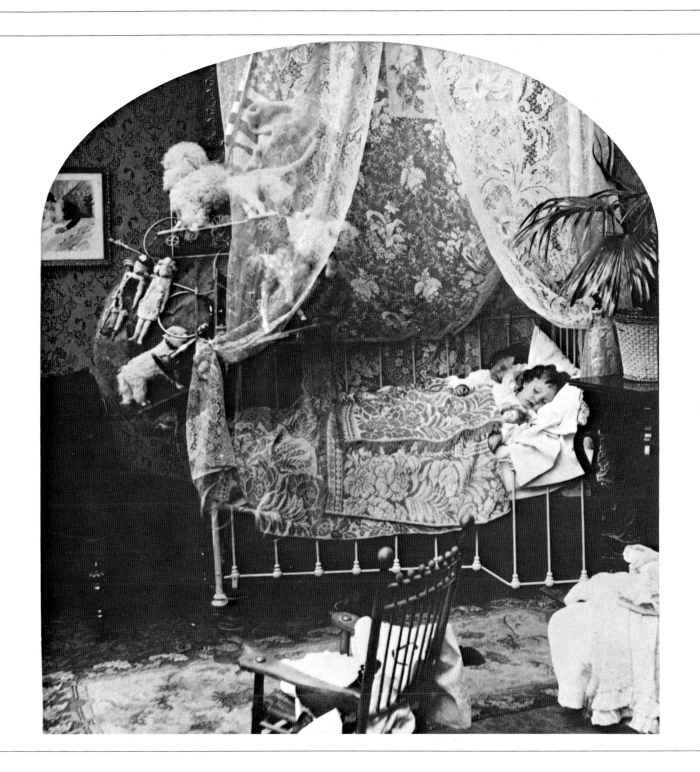

*Designed to hold candy, cornucopias could be made at home according to directions printed in magazines or fancily fringed and trimmed ones, as pictured here, could be purchased at stores, 7¹/₈″-9¹/₂″ h.*

*Opposite page:*

*Paper heads, cards, stars, fish, and cornucopias adorn this Pennsylvania tree at the turn of the century. Courtesy: Fred G. Neece, Jr.*

*Fish, considered both a Christian symbol and a Christmas delicacy in some countries, appeared on the Christmas tree in all shapes and sizes, both handmade and machine made, 7¹/₂″-9¹/₂″ l.*

*With a few sheets of bright colored paper, some pasteboard, some gay tarletan, and a generous supply of popcorn, one may make cornucopias, gold fish, stars, and balls, Christmas fairies, graceful festoons enough to decorate a large tree very handsomely, with an outlay of less than one dollar.*

*Bucks County Intelligencer, December 22, 1874*

church. "Christmas with Variations" in *Peterson's* (1853) gave a glimpse of women making the wreaths and decorating a rural church with roping, tall boughs, and the letters, "IHS", placed in front of the pulpit. The short story also revealed "flushing young cheeks and mysteriously touching hands," proof that the activity was not all work nor all female. Perhaps this is why women's diaries frequently note they are going to help "fix up" for Christmas. Also the occasion is repeatedly used by short story writers for the next three decades; the decorations they describe are similar to ones noted by Anna Garret of Chester County in her 1889 diary, "made wreaths out of evergreens and life everlasting . . . met at our Grange Hall and trimmed up for Christmas. . . ." An excerpt from *Ladies Home Journal* (1888) gave more details:

A pretty effect is brought about by stretching ropes of evergreen from a central point in the ceiling to each corner. A line of festooning running around the building, with large branches massed over each window and door, and trailing evergreens hanging from the chandeliers will give almost any church a holiday aspect. Add to this an arch over the altar, with a cross there, and mottoes of "A Merry Christmas," and "Peace on Earth, Good Will to Man" on the walls, and you will be pretty sure to hear people say, when they gather on Christmas day, "How charming. I had no idea they were going to such trouble and expense." Not being in the secret they do not understand that so much could be brought about with a very limited outlay of money, and those who took part in the work will not feel that they went to too much trouble. The pleasure of the work offsets that.

The article continued with suggestions for the chancel-rail, making it into a low hedge by fastening small evergreen trees to it, while the 1912 *Women's Home Companion* reminded its readers that greens should outline the rail, but should not obstruct the view. It was suggested that jars of "flowers of harmonious kinds could be placed on pedestals along the rail and connected with slender vines or chains of flowers. These same draperies could be extended from the ends of the rail, the choir-pews and the altar to the ceiling where they would meet in hanging baskets of greens and flowers.'' Five years later that same magazine suggested that few flowers should be used for the church except for some white ones on the altar. All decorations should be wholly of the evergreens:

In a church which followed this plan, two good-sized pine trees, perhaps eight feet high, were placed one at each side of the altar, firmly braced, and fastened with invisible wires. From a large star of pine and laurel garlands curved gracefully down and were fastened to the side walls of the chancel. The stem of the lectern was twined with the laurel, which was finished in a handsome bunch combined with pine just under the book rest. The chancel rail was almost hidden by a hedge of small pine trees, wired firmly to the rail. Laurel ropes trimmed the pillars which supported the roof, and above the pillars laurel garlands were festooned along the clerestory windows. The pulpit was simply decorated with the laurel. . . .

Although ideas for the decorations of the church did not appear to change greatly, attitudes did, for this same article proposed that much work was required in following their suggestions and that if ''enough money were raised to purchase florists' laurel the work is much reduced.''

In addition to garlands, flowers, and hedges, mottoes and designs were made to be placed on large walls and over the chancel. The mottoes were usually quotations from the Bible.

Edward Young Cox in *The Art of Garnishing Churches at Christmas and other Festivals,* perhaps the most complete manual on church dressing, gives several pages of appropriate texts. The letters for the motto were made several ways and then fastened to a background of greens or a banner of cloth or paper. One method was to cut the letters from cardboard; then to cover them with red or white flannel, white cotton sprinkled with mica, rice, or fancy gilt papers. A more complicated method was to first form the letters using lath board (substitute inch-wide flat molding); then to cover them with bunches of evergreens, dried flowers (strawflowers, pearly everlasting, immortelles), or individual holly leaves. Perforated zinc was suggested as the background used to anchor the letters and the greens; hardware cloth or chicken wire could be used today.

The designs were substantial shapes formed from the plaster lath and then covered with appropriate material. For the church, stars, crosses, and anchors were commonly suggested as in this article from *Ladies' Home Journal* (1888):

I have prepared several designs which will be found quite easy to work out, and very effective if well done.

The foundation of them is lath. This makes a strong frame and one that can be put together by the boys with but little trouble. You will require a saw, a hammer, and a few slim nails.

Those which can be clinched after driving them through the lath are best, as the clinch makes the frame stronger, and helps to hold the lath in place.

I think there will be no difficulty in understanding how to go to work to make the frames for any of these designs, if the diagrams (page 9) accompanying this article are studied a little. . . .

The star is quite as effective when the evergreen is wound on to the frame as in making festoons. Some cover this design solidly with branches. I do not think the effect as pleasing as when the outlines of the frame are followed, leaving open spaces in the center and points. A cluster of flowers, or berries, or autumn leaves can be used in the center. These stars can be used on large, flat wall-surfaces where it is deemed advisable to break up the monotony of a bare spot with better effect than anywhere else. . . .

Many families came to worship and attend the Sunday school program, the donation parties for the ministers, as well as the benefits or fancy fairs for needed improvements, organs or roofs.

Everyone enjoyed viewing the decorations; however, those adorning the church buildings were admonished in *Ladies Home Journal* (1887): ''. . . Church decoration should differ from home decoration in that it should be simple . . . never straining for effect . . . dignified. . . .'' What was not allowed in the church–mistletoe and exuberance –*was* permitted in the home and weeks before Christmas plans were made to cover arches, window frames, chandeliers, picture frames, mantels, and tables in the hall, the parlor and the dining room with holly, laurel, boxwood, smilax, ivy, yew, asparagus fern, wandering jew, pine, as well as ornamental grasses, berries, and flowers for those of less modest means.

Today's taste considers the Victorian's decorations overdone, but that was indicative of the enthusiasm of the age and the size of the large homes often with twelve-foot ceilings which provided ample space for such extravagance.

*Periods of pride in America produced the red, white, and blue patriotic representations of Columbia and silk flags for use on the Christmas tree, 1⁷/₈"-9¹/₄' h.*

*Opposite page:*

*Excerpts appeared in Nerlich's 1902-3 catalogue. Courtesy: Spinning Wheel.*

*In America the table-top tree soon grew, extending from floor to ceiling by the last quarter of the nineteenth century. Fairies, flags, paper dolls dressed in cotton as well as presents adorn this tinsel and popcorn draped tree. Courtesy: Jim Morrison.*

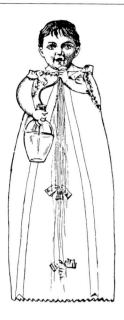

## DOLLS

Lithographed, carved head, arms and feet, fancy ornamented cotton-batting dress.

|  |  | Dozen |
|---|---|---|
| **227/228.** | Assorted, 12 in..1 doz. in pkg.... | $1 20 |
| **230.** | Assorted, Negroes—Boys and Girls, 1 doz. in package................. | 1 20 |
| **231.** | Cat drinking Coffee, dressed, 1 doz. in package................... | 1 20 |
| **346.** | Long dressed baby, 1 doz. in package | 2 20 |
| **345/347.** | Assorted, girl dolls, 16 inch size.. | 2 20 |
| **333.** | Dog smoking pipe, dressed........ | 2 20 |
| **351.** | Santa Claus with tree............ | 2 20 |
| **352.** | Assorted Dolls, 30 inch size........ | 4 00 |

No. 227/228.   $1.20 dozen.

Cornices of greens, leaves, or ferns did not appear heavy over the eighty-inch windows. Also it was the fashion to have a picture molding or ceiling molding from which to hang pictures and this afforded the perfect place to attach garlands. Then pictures hung typically on long chains, ropes, or wires, tilting out from the wall which allowed the mounting of a glass of ivy behind them; the ivy was twined about the frame and hanger. Putting greens behind the family portraits at Christmas was a tribute of remembrance according to *Demorest's* in 1866. Ten years later Annie Hassard in *Floral Decorations* (1876) gave hints to the ladies of the household, whose share it "principally was to make the decoration," for garlands which required scissors, binding-wire, hemp twine, and a pair of strong, but not thick or clumsy, kid gloves:

As has been stated, the best material for the foundation of these is strong hemp cord; a loop should be made on one end, and this is slipped over a nail or hook, fastened for the purpose in a wooden table or in anything that will hold it firmly. Having a supply of evergreens at hand, cut to the required lengths, bind them on to the cord with fine twine–one firm twist of twine will be enough to keep each bunch of evergreens in its place–and so work down the cord to whatever length may be required. A beginner will find it difficult to keep the garland even as it is being worked; but, if such be found to be the case, where it is too full, the pieces can be thinned out with a pair of scissors. If it be desired to suspend a garland of large dimensions at any height, the following shrubs will be found the best adapted for its construction, viz.:–Arbutus, Euonymous (common), Holly, Ivy, Laurel, Portugal Laurel, Spruce, and Silver Firs, and Yew. For giving color, of course, scarlet berries are indispensable, and first amongst these ranks the Holly; . . . . When the berries of this plant can be got, they may be worked in with the evergreens at equal distances, as the formation of the garland is proceeded with; but the best way to arrange the Holly berries is to remove all the leaves and cut off the stems, leaving that portion only which is covered with berries; a piece of fine binding-wire can then be fastened round the stem and passed round the garland, and, where fastened, hid amongst the foliage. In this manner, all the berries can be added after the garland is made.

*Whether rescued from a treasured pencil box or designed especially for the tree, this board, woodburned and painted, was used as an ornament, 12⁷⁄₈″ l.*

*Horseshoes similar to the pink and silver flat-cardboard ornaments pictured here were often seen on trees, 4³⁄₄″-5³⁄₄″ h.*

*Opposite page:*

*These flat-cardboard gold and black lyres might have been drawn from the pattern offered in the 1880 December issue of* Godey's Lady's Book, *7¹⁄₂″ h.*

*In 1902 when Ella Buss came to see cousin Jim Hoover's tree on Walnut Street in Mifflinburg, she found it lavishly covered with flat paper cardboard ornaments. Courtesy: Olive Thompson Hoover.*

Some introduce flowers made of colored tissue-paper, but I myself prefer color being given with berries only. Small and light-looking garlands for suspending from gas brackets, etc., can be made on fine twine, in a similar manner to those before described; but, for this purpose, a very small-leaved plants should be employed, such as the Prickly Holly, variegated Box, etc. . . .

Annie Hassard was also concerned with the dining room, giving examples of decorations for a large table (twelve-foot) and a smaller table (eight-foot). Presumably the hostess that could afford the flowers suggested for this eight-foot table had servants for there was no room on the table for serving dishes. The center of the table was reserved for a March stand which was a three-tiered flower arranger, approximately twenty inches tall, the top being a trumpet-shaped vase. The bottom dish, after being lined with fern fronds, was filled with ivy, white chrysanthemums, scarlet geraniums, Larustinus, holly berries, white lilac, and maiden-hair fern. Variegated ivy was twisted up the stem to the second tier where more geraniums, jonquils (white), or any other white and scarlet flowers were arranged with maiden-hair fern. Cascading out of the trumpet-shaped vase on top were ornamental grasses, ferns, light-looking scarlet and white flowers, and leaves of wavy, graceful pampas grass. Around the stand were arranged eight specimen glasses. Four of normal height and four shorter ones were filled with an assortment of the flowers and plants used in the stand. At each end of the table should be a Jerusalem Cherry in an ornamental pot, the soil covered with moss and three dried pods of Roast-Beef Plant (Iris fostidissma). (It should be noted that upper-class homes of this period were designed with conservatories or indoor greenhouses.) White and black grapes should be in a bowl at the head of the table, apples at the foot. "Pears, nuts, figs, etc." should be arranged on both sides. Additional table arrangements and directions for a March stand can be found in Sunny O'Neil's *The Gift of Christmas Past* (1981).

*. . . all the beautiful ornaments were made by the family—the paper decorations being the handiwork of Mrs. Sener. These consist of fairies, gondolas, boots, slippers, harps, musical lyres, baskets, stars, chains, and what not!*

Lancaster Evening Express, *December 28, 1875*

The next year, 1876, *Ladies' Home Journal* again makes the distinction between church and home decorations, the introduction of color: flags, ribbon, sashes, fans, banners, and India shawls being mingled with the greens at home. This was the only mention of bows–one of red satin tied on a wreath–found in the magazines read. *Demorest's* again describes household decorations in 1878. Home-made hanging baskets of pasteboard covered with moss and filled with drooping evergreens such as myrtle could be adapted to archways, chandeliers, the center of the ceiling, or, if constructed with flat backs, placed directly against the wall. A "Welcome" motto covered with gilt paper would serve for the archway in the hall. Pressed oak leaves and

*This jewel casket is presumed to have been made by Helen Burrowes of Milton in the 1880s, 5" h.*

*Drawn on cardboard, cut, covered with red glazed paper, then trimmed with silver tinsel, this owl once hooted from a Christmas tree in Muncy, Pennsylvania, 8³/₈" h.*

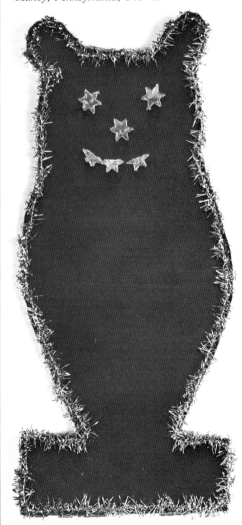

bunches of acorns formed circular wreaths that were varnished and handsome; gay, elegant wreaths of bittersweet provided color.

Ten years later, in *Our Homes* (1888) David W. Judd was still recommending the ivy as "capital material for wreaths around pictures as well as bittersweet." He found the princess-pine and ground-pine excellent for wreaths and roping for they "do not drop." Banners and mottoes are still in style but he warns that in a small room the work on the banner must be nice for it is more conspicuous. The large and roomy halls, "as halls should be," requires wreaths above each picture, groups of flags on the wall, and sprays of evergreens fastened to laths over the doors. The door to the dining room should be garlanded with greens and bittersweet. Over the dining-room mantel near the ceiling could be fastened a "large bunch of green mixed with wheat, millet and berries" from which vines or ropes of green would "hang down and be fastened out at each side." And in 1891 the *Ladies' Home Journal* advised that "Christmas would seem incomplete were green decoration left out. Even the poor woman who lives in one or two rooms in some dirty tenement house will save money enough to buy a few bits of holly. Greens should be purchased at the market when they are first brought in and then taken home and put in the cellar and sprinkled with water. It is better not to put them up until the afternoon before Christmas." Holly was thought most appropriate for the hall, sitting-room, dining-room, and library. However, ivy was still the best for twining around picture frames; "fifty cents' worth of the green stuff called 'Wandering Jew' " would fill several bowls and vases and, if well cared for, would keep for months. Large dishes of holly and laurel should be placed in the fireplaces if a fire was not planned (stoves must have been present for heating). Smilax, asparagus fern and other delicate vines were appropriate for pictures and statuary but since the article was written for people with

modest purses, a hardy wild fern which sold for "ten cents a dozen sprays" was the suggestion for these places as well as the dining room table.

If all the suggestions offered had been heeded surely every home would have resembled the one described in the *Delineator* in 1893:

The lower hall and rooms had been converted into perfect bowers of cedar, fir, holly box and

mistletoe, and interspersed among the dark-green leaves were numerous glittering tinsel ornaments and silvered glass balls, such as the Germans are fond of using for their Christmas decorations.

In addition, there were many fairy lamps of colored glass which were hung here and there among the garlands and festoons adorning the walls and entwining the stair-rail. Tiny wicks floating in sperm oil burned in these pretty glasses and emitted a soft, mellow light that charmed the vision and made one think of a gala night in fairy-land. Unique chandeliers formed of wooden frames and hoops were covered with evergreens and held waxen candles, and fairy lamps were also suspended from their framework.

On the walls of the halls and parlors were inscriptions, suitable to the season, wrought in

Dozen

**103.** Child figures, 1 doz. in box . . . . . . . . . . . . . . . $0 70
**112.** Angel figures, 1 doz. in box . . . . . . . . . . . . . . 0 70
**106.** Cherub heads, 2 doz. in box . . . . . . . . . . . . . . 0 70
**208.** Angels and Cherubs in flower frame, 1 doz. in package . . . . . . . . . . 0 80
**214.** Bethlehem scenes . . . 0 80
**301.** Cherub heads (large), 1 doz. in package . . . . . 1 00
**307.** Angel group, 1 doz. in package . . . . . . . . . . 1 00
**308.** Cherub figures, 1 doz. in package . . . . . . . . . . 1 00
**403.** Santa Claus, 1 doz. in package . . . . . . . . . . 1 50
**505.** Ideal Child bust with rich wreath of roses, 1 doz. in package . . . . . . 2 00

*Nerlich's 1902 catalog listing.*

evergreens and lighted with fairy lamps. Among them were *A Merry Xmas, On Earth Peace Good Will Toward Men, In Christmas Greeting,* and *God rest you, merrie gentlemen, Let nothing you dismay.* On the end wall of the back parlor was a large star of evergreens. . . .

Life became much simpler or the readership of the women's periodicals changed, for table decorations, although still considered important by the editors, became more modest. Those recommended were generally of home manufacture and thematic, including place-cards and favors. For example, Katherine Parker, a writer for *Good Housekeeping* in 1904 described the plans a woman (albeit one with a maid) devised for her dinner party for eight. She discarded the idea of a tree for she had used it last year, poinsettias because they were not available in her town, holly because it was too expensive and ribbons made it more so, as well as an arrangement of red carnations and asparagus fern because it was not Christmasy. She

settled on constructing the north pole. Using a mirror for the base, she placed a shallow tin pan in the center, filled it with a block of ice on which stood a mailing tube "covered with white glazed paper; touched with mucilage and dazzling with diamond dust." Cotton wadding was piled around the base of the ice, concealing the tin pan, and "rock candy icebergs glittered on the snow." Some sprigs of holly had been dusted with the diamond dust or mica; others had been dipped into an alum solution so crystals had formed on the leaves. A tiny white toy bear stood near the pole and a doll dressed like an "Esquimau" completed the scene. Additional sprigs of holly were affixed to the chandelier and borrowed prisms "hung from it like icicles." Crepe paper was used to cover the glass globes and paper shades softened the light of the candles. The dessert carried out the theme for it was cake and snowballs, ice cream rolled into balls and covered with coconut. At each plate was a cardboard sled she made and filled with a box of candy.

For the general decoration of the house she used the lengths of ground pine that can be bought in the market very cheaply after the crowd has thinned on Christmas Eve. A quarter has large possibilities and fifty cents buys a wealth of it. Over the door leading from the hall she fastened it in pointed Moorish arches, catching it in the center at the top and letting it frame the sides. And in the long hall swung a fragrant swinging curtain of equal lengths of the green, like a Japanese bead portiere.

Almost all of the people interviewed in central Pennsylvania remember mother's best bowl holding greens at the center of the table, but Bee Petrie, whose earliest memory goes back ninety years, fastened ground pine and princess pine over the mantels and chandeliers as well as the pictures, all gathered from the woods by the family. Although many remembered the various smells and tastes of the Christmas feast few recalled household decorations. Therefore, it can be assumed that rural homes never emulated the lavish decorations of the aforementioned magazines.

Although the subject of church and household decorations was a popular feature of the periodicals in the 1870s the tree, now considered the symbol of the holiday, was not. There is some controversy about when and where the first decorated tree appeared in America, but it is generally accepted that the custom came from Germany. In Ammerschweir, Alsace in 1561 a forest ordinance declared that "no burgher shall have for Christmas more than one bush of more than eight shoes length." Since trees were not as abundant in Europe as in America, most European trees remained small, and some were actually formed by attaching greens to a frame. This pyramid custom was introduced into America by the Moravians and was described in a diary entry for December 25, 1745. However, the use of a live tree was more common and several states claim to have had the first, Pennsylvania among them. Authors, Phillip V. Snyder and Alfred Shoemaker document the development of the tree in this country.

The public or community tree custom was begun as early as 1830 in York, Pennsylvania, and admission was charged. Using the tree to raise funds was a tradition which continued, for the *Mifflinburg Telegraph* reports "twenty cents for adults, ten cents for children" were required for admission to the Laurelton Reformed Church on December 24, 1880 to see the tree and the Sunday school program. The church was raising money for a new organ. A. N. Squires of Harrisburg wrote in his diary on December 25, 1895, "not going to [see a] Christmas tree as we are ready to have one ourselves."

Oral tradition in Union/Snyder counties supports the importance of the Sunday school tree; some families took their presents to Sunday school to have them distributed. Some families, however, had their own tree; those that did not such as Clara Williamson's of Chester County, enjoyed their friend's. From Clara's diary we learn that in 1863 she went to Marsha Hall's house to see the Christmas tree lighted

and returned the next year to "fix" the tree. In 1864 and 1865 she trimmed Alice Dillingham's and Janey Waddell's. The Danville *Intelligencer* remarks on January 4, 1877, "Beautiful Christmas trees are visible to passers by through the windows of several residences in the borough." The tree and its decorations were described in short stories in leading periodicals of the day as in *Godey's* December 1860 issue. It was, however not until the 1880s that *Godey's Lady's Book* gave specific directions for "planting" the tree and making decorations. The other magazines followed the lead of *Godey's* editor, Sarah Hale, and offered their suggestions during the next two decades.

Beginning in the 1890s, novel substitutes were presented for dispensing the gifts: giant stockings, hampers, or grandmother's pockets as well as wands, spider webs, and mock orange trees. Designs were also shown for space-saving frames for walls and for over the mantel which were deemed necessary by "crowded flats and busy mothers" who presumably had no space or time for trees. Ironically the tree had originally developed as a substitute dispenser of gifts–gradually replacing the plates, caps, bran pies, and stockings used by earlier generations.

It is evident that the tree, as a bearer of gifts, existed earlier than the 1880-1900 period when it receives marked emphasis in the period literature. Harriet Beecher Stowe writes to her father Calvin Stowe on December 22, 1850 from Brunswick, Maine:

Our Christmas tree was a fine spruce and when it sat on the table it touched the wall, and I made four gilt stars for the four top branches and ma dressed a little doll like a fairy in white with gilt spangles & a gilt band around her head & a star on her forehead & a long gilt wand with a star on the end & gause wings spangled with gold she was placed in the tree with her wand pointing to the presents on it & there was no end to the gilt apples and nuts etc.

In 1864, Madame Demorest of *Demorest's Illustrated Monthly* was reported by the *New York Tribune* as having invited "over one hundred and sixty of the young ladies employed" to her residence on East Fourteenth Street "to

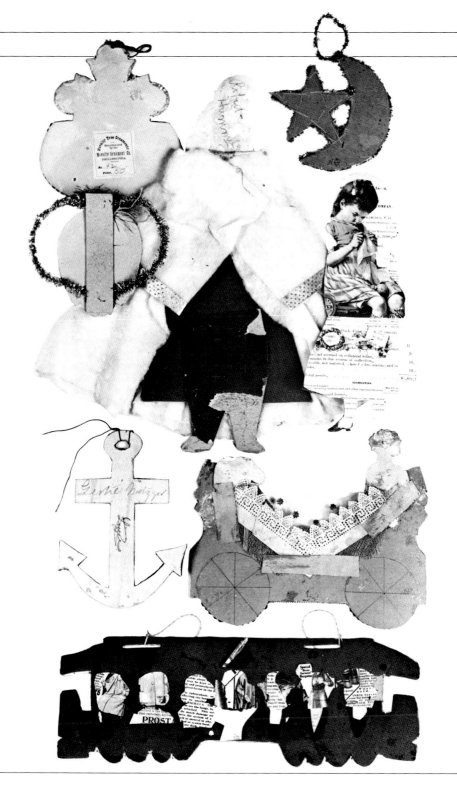

*Opposite page:*
*Assembled from tradecards and scrap reliefs, homemade and handmade paper dolls were clothed in tissue and crepe paper for use on the Christmas tree, 5"-8¼" h.*

*Backs of ornaments offer many clues to their age, manufacturer, and ownership: the upper left are commercially manufactured, the remainder were made for personal use, 4"-8¼" h.*

view a gigantic Christmas tree, laden with a large number of costly presents which were distributed by lot, each visitor receiving one.'' In 1874 the *Muncy Luminary* (Muncy, Pennsylvania) on December twelfth had this to say:

The size of the Christmas tree depends on the number of presents it is to be laden with; for a Sunday-school one or sometimes two trees of quite large size are procured. They may be of pine, hemlock, cedar, arbor vitae, or spruce; any evergreen of suitable shape will answer the purpose. The tree is usually set in a box and firmly fastened in place, the box is covered with white paper or muslin, prettily decorated with greenery, and serves as a resting place for presents too heavy to be hung on the tree. Popcorn strung may be gracefully twined in festoons on the tree; ornamental balls of various colors of shiny surface come on purpose for decoration; also small wax candles with tin candlesticks which are fastened to the tree with wire; also miniature flags, cornucopias of brilliant tints and filled with candies are pleasing to the children. Eggs from which the contents have been carefully removed may be covered with bits of gilt paper cut from the band of envelopes, with flowers or fancy shapes cut out of calico or silk or any highly colored material and pasted on–these suspended from the limbs add beauty to the tree. Red and scarlet apples look well. The presents are labeled with the name of the persons for whom they are intended and hung upon the tree. The distribution takes place after the feast which it crowns and closes; the lighting of the candles in the tree giving the final effect to its beauty, before the gifts are removed.

Frimom these sample descriptions, some conclusions can be made. The tree was the holder of the presents. Toward the end of the century, some writers deplored this custom for they claimed that removing the gifts ruined the appearance of the tree. As the practice of gift giving increased until there were complaints of the holiday ''degenerating into a festival of store-keepers,'' perhaps the tree could no longer hold the tokens of affection so laboriously planned and made in the earlier years. If

*Elegantly attired in paper-lace and carrying her red and gold cardboard umbrella, this paper lady might be visiting friends in their red paper-lace curtained cardboard mansion, 2⅝″-4⅝″ h.*

this were true and the tree was not to be "plucked" by the children, the decorations could become more elaborate.

Candles were used on the tree, as unsafe and impractical as it appeared. In fact only one editor *dared* suggest that they should not be used when there are paper ornaments. The others recommended that a pail of water be kept nearby, a person with a sponge on a stick should be appointed to watch the tree or, most original, a long blow pipe should be provided to blow out the candles as they "became refractory" or burned close to the tree.

One of the first decorations described was a candy container, a cornucopia. Although as early as 1877 one could purchase four sizes of cornucopias from *Ehrich's Fashion Quarterly* (the smallest size was thirty-five cents a dozen) directions were given in most periodicals for making cornucopias such as in *Demorest's* (1890):

Pretty cornucopias may be made . . . by cutting out triangles of cardboard in any desired size, and covering them with colored paper. Sew the shortest edges together, round off the top, cover with gold, silver, red, or blue paper. Finish the top with paper lace and a band of gilt paper, and fasten a wire hook to it to hang it up by. Make larger cornucopias . . . of squares of cardboard covered in the same way.

Another method is to draw and cut an eleven inch circle from fancy paper. Draw and cut a twelve inch circle from white paper. Cut both circles into six equal parts. Place the fancy paper on top of the white paper, allowing the white to extend over the top. Glue the papers together, sliding a narrow ribbon for a handle, between outside and inside sheets. Form into a cone and glue, ornamenting with fringe, ruffles, fancy pictures as you desire. (*The Delineator, 1901*)

Besides the cornucopia, readers could make small, shaped bags of netting or the pretty stockings of coarse Brussels net described in *Good Housekeeping* (1896):

They are quickly made as all can be cut out at once and simply put together with a coarse buttonhole stitch all around the edge, with various colored worsteds. A piece of worsted or baby ribbon drawn around the top acts as draw string. Fill with brightly colored candies and they will make a pretty and inexpensive adornment to your tree.

*The Youth's Companion* (December 18, 1879) gave directions for cardboard candy containers shaped and decorated to resemble drums and muffs; at the top of the drum and the ends of the muff were glued pieces of tarlatan that had a drawstring closing as did some of the manufactured paper candy containers. The tarlatan, an unwashable, stiff, transparent muslin, used for the drawstring tops of the candy containers, was also shaped into stockings, mittens, socks, shoes, or other fanciful shapes and filled with sugar plums and hung on the tree. Commercial examples were machine-stitched, but homemade ones were whip stitched or buttonholed by hand. A collection of tarlatan ornaments (p. 32) was purchased in the Danville area approximately fifteen years ago, selected from a larger, presumably, family collection of ornaments. Made from trade cards, they appear to be stitched by the same hand. The square envelope pocket was trimmed with a sandpaint advertisement exhibiting a patent date of 1896.

*There is a certain charm about Christmas that does not attach to any other holiday . . .*

*Middleburgh Post,* December 22, 1881

Even though these candy containers were made locally and area residents considered homemade candy essential to the celebration, few remembered candy containers on the tree. Only a few candy canes and "clear toys" decorated the boughs of Union/Snyder trees in the first decade of the twentieth century.

The "sugar or clear toys" were made by pouring a boiled mixture of barley sugar and water into greased metal molds shaped like animals, toys, babies, and Santas. The candy would harden, and when removed, if it had been prepared properly, it would be transparent. These red, yellow, and green jewel-like shapes could be hung on the tree or slowly sucked, giving great pleasure to the recipient. Most often the "clear toys" were purchased rather than homemade. The product perhaps

*Gowned in paper lace, crepe and tissue paper, these ornaments were meant to dance on the tips of the tree branches, 8"-9½" h.*

Advertising calendars provided the heads for dolls which were dressed for the tree in many households in the Union/Snyder area, 8½" h.

The angel on the left has a scrap relief head and commercially pressed cardboard wings, while her mate is fashioned from a Lyons Coffee advertising doll and sprouts foil covered wings, 7⁵/₁₆" h.

was limited geographically to the New York, Pennsylvania, and Maryland area for when Tasha Tudor illustrated trees decorated with the "toys", orders came from all over the country to Keithan's in Sunbury and Murrays' in Watsontown, many accompanied with the notation that the person was not familiar with the products, but wanted to see them since they appeared so delightful.

The other favorite of the children, hard candies, seem to come from a generous school teacher or from the Sunday school festival in small rectangular boxes. Also, popcorn draped in festoons (loops) has been used for many years; however, variations of pinning single kernels on the branches to imitate snow, tinting the popcorn red and green before stringing, making of popcorn balls for the tree, and later, purchasing popcorn balls wrapped in colored cellophane for the tree all appear in interviews and descriptions of family activities in this area.

Another item of note is the use of fruit on the tree, often apples, which were believed to be a hold-over from the time of the paradise tree in the street plays when the story of Adam and Eve was dramatized. Some descriptions called for "lady apples" which were smaller. Most rural families would have had apples in the root cellar and the color would have been a pleasing addition. Although apples were mentioned frequently as decorations for the tree by many publications, only one, *Good Housekeeping* (1899), named the orange which was regarded by many area informants as indispensible to the celebration, for it was usually the only time they received one during the year. The word "fruit" in descriptions of trees can also refer to the gifts and the fancy decorations as well and should not always be taken literally.

Decorations should include "tiny flags, costing but a trifle per dozen," which were mentioned as ornaments and which can be seen in many early photographs of trees. (In fact, they are one way to identify the origin of the tree and possibly the date.) They become more popular during periods of intense patriotism such as the Mexican War (1848), the War Between the States (1861-1865), the Spanish-American

*After using their purchased Christmas tree the first year, frugal German families would strip the needles and wrap the limbs in cotton thereby extending its use for several years. The honeycomb streamer and tinsel-wrapped ornaments suggest an early 1900 date for this tree. Courtesy: Jim Morrison.*

*Women and children made the paper ornaments and trimmed the glass ones whether for home use or for cottage industries here and in Germany. Courtesy: Library of Congress.*

*Horns toot and bells ring as the sleighs dash across the snow, an eagerly anticipated social event portrayed here in paper ornaments, 7″ – 9″ h.*

*Opposite page:*
*Victorias, cabriolets, and trolleys were stylish means of transportation when these ornaments were made. The smaller homemade hot-air balloon dates to 1881; the sailboat was patented in 1878, 11¼″ longest, 12″ highest.*

*I went to Phila on Xmas eve & stayed three days. . . As large & fine a tree as can be accommodated being procured & set up, it is covered with every conceivable shape into which coloured & gilt paper & card can be cut, and . . . little pictures, glass balls, chains, garlands &c . . . there was a very handsome river steamboat—perfect—3 feet long with about 50 passengers (these last small pictures cut out) all of white, coloured & gilt card. Also a beautifull fire hose carriage.*

January 20, 1876, John Lewis Letters
Collection of Regional History,
Cornell University

*Circled in their skirts of tarlatan, these seven ladies and a young boy were possibly handmade according to the directions in* Harper's Bazar, *1887, 5³/₈″-9¹/₄″ h.*

War (1898), and WWI (1917-1918). The Centennial Exposition (1875) as well as the Columbian (1893) were also periods of great pride in America which is reflected in some ornaments (p. 16).

"Shiny ornamental balls for the purpose" undoubtedly meant glass Christmas balls which would have been available in some areas for, according to Malcolm Rogers, collector and researcher, records support the existence of a glass manufacturer named Adolphus W. De-

muth in New York City about 1864. *Ehrich's Fashion Quarterly* (1876) offered glass balls from one inch to one and one-half inches in diameter at the cost of sixty-five cents, plus nine cents mailing, for a box of the smallest size containing one hundred forty-four ornaments, and Maggie Rogers, in *The Glass Christmas Ornament* (1977), noted that New York and New Jersey glass-makers were blowing kugel-like ornaments in the 1880s. Only one other article of those read suggested glass

balls as "a nice addition to the tree, expensive but one that can be saved."

The use of egg shells on the trees described by the 1874 *Muncy Luminary* was not unique. Two years later, an account in the *Lancaster Examiner and Express* reported that "sixty blown-shells painted by Dr. M. L. Herr were used for the decoration of his tree. Eva Stille in *Christbaumschmuck* (1979) noted that in the nineteeth century recent German immigrants to Texas, upon finding themselves in the "wild west" at Christmas and having only brought their favorite angel for the top of their tree as well as some gold and silver tinsel, depended on their grandmother to fashion ornaments by pasting pieces of material and the tinsel to egg shells. The popularity of the egg at Christmas continued into the 1890s:

The little flower-basket is made of a blown eggshell glued to the upper side of a large wooden button-mold, which is then gilded. The egg basket is filled with moss and flowers. . . .
  Egg-shells painted and decorated as illustrated, also make very pretty Christmas-tree ornaments. The pearl of these is one decorated with a moss landscape and a scene of the Nativity in hair-line silhouettes. Here is a chance for the artist in black-and-white. (*Demorest's* 1890)

Now, mama always uses several dozen eggs at Christmas time, so beg the privilege of blowing out the contents and leaving the shells unbroken. Five or six dozen will be none too many.

Paint some a bright yellow, some blue, some light-green (dark green will not show), and at least half with different shades of red, as these latter are very effective. When dry, run a wire through them and fasten them on the tree. (*Good Housekeeping*, 1895)

Fairies and angels–tiny and tall, flat and dimensional–made from dolls or scrap reliefs hung on the boughs. Harriet Beecher Stowe, daughter of the novelist, described to her father a home-dressed doll on the tree. They were obviously a familiar sight, for several magazine editors of the period lamented the fact that though the angels should be there, they "come rather shabbily dressed which can be easily remedied." Laura Walter (Mifflin-

burg resident) always had an angel at the top of her tree for it just was not Christmas without it. Although many of the dolls dangling from the branches were actual toys (p. 17) there is reason to believe that paper fairies, "just for pretty," flitted among the boughs. When used in Union/Snyder counties "fairies" means any ornament comprised of a pretty picture often backed by cotton and surrounded with tinsel. Good examples are the ornaments made by Olive and Myrtle Thompson's mother, Margaret Minerva, for their tree in 1879 (p. 44). Fairies appear regularly in period photographs of rural Christmas trees. However, the nineteenth century periodicals used the term to mean a child's or female's head and/or figure:

Fairies add greatly to the beauty of the tree; half-length figures can be cut out of colored fashion-plates in illustrated magazines. Feet must be cut out and added, attached to the back of the tarlatan skirt [p. 30]. Great ingenuity can be exercised in dressing these, fancy costumes being selected if desired. Tarlatan, in varied

*Sweet babies were a Victorian delight. The lines on the second tub were printed and the high chair is machine-embossed paper, suggesting that these two ornaments were commercially produced. The high chair and unattended baby carriage are one of a pair, 3³/₄"-7¹/₄" h.*

colors, is used for dressing them, elaborately trimmed with gold and silver lace and spangles. (*Peterson's* 1888)

Now we must have some fairies. If there are any young ladies in the house they must be pressed into the service. If not, then mamma's busy fingers will surely help. Take the little German pictures of children's heads, sew on two or three little tarlatan skirts, which may be trimmed with tinsel or silver stars, and suspend them from the tree by a thread. (*Good House-keeping,* 1895)

Not calling them fairies but describing the same type of decoration *Harpers Bazar* in 1887 suggested dressing lovely facés in skirt after skirt of tarlatan to represent ballet dancers and

adding arms and waists when needed. *Demorest's* in 1890 suggested using cutouts from picture cards and making the skirts of white swiss, adding gilt paper-star crowns and wings (p. 30). *Godey's* in 1888 proposed "gumming embossed scrap heads on to an oblong piece of cardboard: fasten on some wire arms, the ends of which should be turned round and covered with pieces of an old kid glove" and continued with ideas for dressing them as "aborigines of all nations."

In addition to fairies and angels, other figures embellished the tree, one being paper dolls (pp. 24, 25, and 45). Although according to Marion Howard in *Those Fascinating Paper Dolls* (1981), paper dolls were printed in this country

as early as 1812 and Dennison's paper dolls became popular in the 1880s, there are few printed references to their use on the tree. Dennison catalogs studied at Winterthur suggest the paper doll for a lampshade or chandelier ornament but not for the tree. Only *The Standard Designer* (1896) advises: "Paper dolls with jointed limbs can be bought for a few cents apiece, and may be dressed in a variety of ways: some of them even make very pretty Christmas angels when decked out with tissue paper wings and the floating robes of pale blue or pink with gilt stars for trimming." They continue by noting that the dolls (four to fourteen inches tall) make the tree bright but also provide acceptable gifts for little girls if outfit-

*Tarlatan, a thin, stiff muslin, transparent and unwashable, was used for this handmade collection. The envelope (second from the right) is decorated with a figure cut from a paint advertisement patented in 1896, 5"-3³/₄" h.*

*Opposite page:*

*Manufactured paper dolls and paper and tinsel ornaments dangle from the branches of this tree while the Christmas house nestles beneath it upon a field of cotton. Courtesy: Jeannette Lasansky.*

ted with clothes that can be removed "at will" and accompanied by a few sheets of colored paper to replenish the wardrobe as needed. In addition to the home-dressed paper dolls in tissue and crepe paper (pp. 22 and 25) were dolls dressed in cotton batting offered by catalogues similar to *Ehrich's Fashion Quarterly* and Sears Roebuck and Company; they could be ordered in a variety of sizes (approximately four to eighteen inches) and scrap-relief faces (babies, young ladies and Santas) but all similarly dressed. The cotton batting clothes were trimmed with bands and bows of crepe paper, often cut with pinking shears, and almost always had a scalloped edge (p. 45).

If two, five or ten cents was too much to pay, charming dolls could be fashioned at home from calendars (p. 26), trade-cards (p. 23), catalogs, and magazines (p. 23). One of the angels (p. 26) from the Roat family of Washingtonville has a price, two cents, marked on the back and is definitely made from a scrap head and machine pressed wings. Even its tinsel is applied so deftly as to make it appear commercial although family tradition credits grandmother, Violetta Jane Dietrich Roat, with making it for her first tree in the 1880-90s. She also assembled one from a Lyon's coffee advertising doll and homemade silver wings, embroidering it along the same lines as the tinsel of its mate. Other snowmaidens, obviously homemade appear (p. 44), but none of the "miniature snow men," shaped from a bunch of cotton and coated with alum, with nose and eyes of charcoal, and topped with a gilt hat, as described in *Demorest's* (1890), were found. Other handmade, but not homemade cotton figures exist marked "Germany" and "Japan". They are nevertheless, women's handicraft for most of the paper and cotton ornaments, and even the decorations on the glass shapes were done in cottage industries by women and children (p. 27).

According to Christa Pieska in *Volkunst,* the early scraps were manufactured also by women or sometimes prisoners, working in German factories. The work was hard but required patience and skill. The scraps were run through the presses as many as twenty-six times for the

colors then coated with a gelatin or varnish. They were dried and re-coated and re-dried, embossed by a power machine, and finally, stamped out, twenty-five sheets at a time. More intricate designs required hand cutting; gilding was another separate process. Almost all of the workers on scraps received substantial wages for the period, and fancy papers were a contributing factor to the economy of Germany where most of the printing was done even for French and English firms. About 1875 typical firms like Hagelberg and Albrecht & Meister began to mass produce the embossed, diecut pictures known as scraps, scrap reliefs and chromolithographs (chromos); the latter term is misleading for it refers to a process which was used for printing rather than the die-cuts themselves. First introduced in this country in the 1860s by the valentine trade, their popularity increased about the time of the Philadelphia Exposition. The scraps were scenes of homelife, children playing, fashion ladies, animals, fruits, and baskets of flowers. At the peak of their popularity more than five thousand subjects were featured. The colorful scraps captured the hearts and hands of women here and in England, and by the 1880s no home could be without its "scrapbook", a carefully arranged collection of the pictures. English firms like Mamelok and Raphael Tuck also used scraps for creating educational toys, another popular Victorian pastime. From the earlier Valentine market, scraps of nymphs, flowers, and springlike images found their way to the Christmas tree, either alone or in combination with cotton, tinsel, crepe paper, and celluloid (p. 35). Some figures were as tall as fifteen inches, but most scraps were fitted on sheets or swags approximately nine and one-half inches by twelve and one-half inches and the number contained on each sheet varied from two to hundreds depending on the size of the scrap. The scrap angel heads were most frequently seen (p. 34), but the flowers and children, in particular, made their appearance on collections of flat paper ornaments. Later scraps were designed specifically for the Christmas market producing an array of Father Christmases and snow children (p. 34).

*The most popular motifs found on the tree were santas and angels. They were usually affixed to cardboard shapes covered in all hues of cotton, crepe, or glazed paper, 3$^1$/$_2$" - 10" h.*

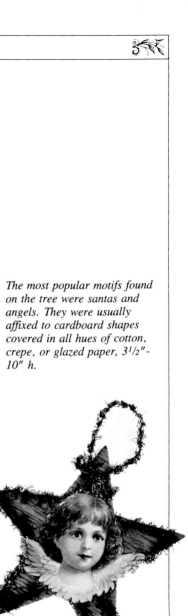

About 1881 with "Gold and Silver Papers, Col'd Glazed Paper, Gold and Silver Stars" as advertised by Evans's University Bookstore in the *Lewisburg Chronicle* (December 8, 1881) in hand, Helen Burrowes, who lived in nearby Milton, began creating flat paper ornaments for her two daughters' tree. Possibly the patterns were inspired by the December 1880 article printed in *Godey's Lady's Book* or could have been copies of "store bought" ones like the sailboat (p. 29) which has "W. G. and Co., P. Pending, September, 1878" printed on the back. Over the years she, and perhaps her daughters, may have added to the collection for thirty-seven ornaments were preserved; one, a balloon, has 1881 printed on the catalog model used for a rider in the gondola (p. 29). Other collections of flat paper ornaments have

survived, made by the Metzger family in the Lancaster area, as well as by the Nuss family in Muncy, however none of these ornaments have dates. The subject matter of these three family collections is similar: shoes, vases, baskets, pitchers, urns and lyres providing a delightful glimpse of the styles of the day (pp. 18, 36, 37, and 40). There is also a variety of stars, hearts, and anchors (pp. 38 and 39) like those mentioned in the *Godey's* article. The ornaments are very similar to "fairies, gondolas, boots, slippers, harps, musical lyres, baskets, stars, chains, and what not; and all of such good size and rich contrast of color" described and dated 1874-1877 in Shoemaker's Christmas in Pennsylvania (1959). To say that they are simply-made does not credit the originator with the taste and patience required to trim the shapes once cut from cardboard and covered with glazed paper, or as cited in the contemporary articles, fire gilt for the sparkle of the tree was

all-important since it was lit only briefly by candles.

A public collection of flat paper ornaments can be seen at the William Penn Museum in Harrisburg. It was purchased approximately forty years ago from an antique dealer and is not known to be from one family, but it remains an excellent array both of the colors and materials used and the forms and sizes of paper ornaments which were popular from 1874-1920. All appear to be hand assembled although two have a manufacturer's mark, the sailboat and a covered dish stamped "A Novelty Tree Ornament Manufactured by the Novelty Ornament Company, Philadelphia" (p. 23). Unfortunately a search of Philadelphia City Directories by Grace Wozniak of the Pennsylvania Historical and Museum Commission did not reveal the presence of this firm before 1900. A subsequent search of the Manufacturer's Census for 1880 revealed only a

*Commercially produced colored pictures known as glanzbilders, scraps, or scrap reliefs were surrounded with tinsel, gold paper, and celluloid for the embellishment of the tree, 3³/₄"-9¹/₄" h.*

*Reproduced in flat cardboard, baskets and bowls were fancied by the ladies for elegant tree ornaments in silver, black, pale green, and pink as well as red, 4"-8⁷/₈" h.*

Novelty Box Company specializing in fancy paper; Philadelphia City Directories placed the company at 440 North 12th Street in 1885 and in 1895 but it was no longer there by 1901. Whether it was the producer of the ornament and others like it is impossible to say; fancy box manufacturers certainly would have had the necessary supplies. Commercial handmade ornaments were possibly manufactured like the dolls, favors, and mottoes (crackers) handled later by C. A. Reed/Westvaco of Williamsport. Materials, pre-cut and measured, were distributed by the gross at locations in Hughesville, Muncy, Newberry, Montgomery, and Jersey Shore to women who would return finished products the following week. They would be paid forty to eighty-three cents per gross, and if the work was neat, would receive more supplies. This practice continued until Pennsylvania labor laws forbade cottage work in the 1930s, forcing such workers into factories.

*The recent rage for fancy paper and card ornaments has utterly died out, and sugar and crystal have taken their place, with small imitation silver and gold conceits of various designs to supply the glitter.*

Bucks County Intelligencer, December 23, 1882

These towns would not have had the company listed in directories unless a factory was established there. Wherever it was made, the ornament, "No. 42," priced at fifty cents, was a luxury item at the time, for the average wage earner in the 1890s working fifty to sixty hours a week earned little more than twelve dollars a week. A quart of milk cost six cents, a pound of roundsteak, twelve cents, and ladies' periodicals reported that a dollar's worth of trinkets–opera glasses, peacocks, lanterns–would be sufficient to dress even a large tree. In the Union/Snyder area, residents repeatedly declared that they did not have store-bought ornaments on their trees for "they cost money", so homemade items, mostly paper, were the popular accouterments.

The use of the flat paper cutouts described by a Lancaster newspaper editor in 1875 as "most fashionable" grew with encouragement from numerous periodicals like *Harper's Bazar*. So popular had handmade paper ornaments become that the *Ladies Home Journal* pronounced them trite and useless in 1887:

Have no paper articles on the tree, except receptacles made to hold something, as bonbons. Fancy boxes, baskets, and cornucopias are allowable, but the time wasted over chains, gondolas, tinsel ornaments in recent years, has been something fearful to contemplate. Real dressed dolls look more sensible than caricature fairies or angels, as they can be used; besides which, they are likely to be more beautiful.

. . . Cover a bare spot by a Japanese fan which, if paper, is paper put to a use.

This declamation by the *Journal* had little effect, for *Peterson's* the following year told readers to make a red firegilt heart pierced by a golden arrow, and *Demorest's* in 1890 noted that Greek Latin, and Maltese crosses are all shapes that make pretty souvenirs, and ornaments for the tree (p. 10). *Harper's* editors continued the fervor, remarking in 1891:

Many showy ornaments may be made at home. Cut from common pasteboard a number of different forms, such as hearts, crosses, anchors, crescents, stars, etc., brush them on both sides with liquid glue, and then dip them in a bowl filled with sand, sawdust, mustard-seed or pounded rice, or with a mixture of two or more of these ingredients. When this rough coat is perfectly dry, color the forms with any of the metallic or enamel paints, thus completing very rich decorations. . . .

In 1899 *Good Housekeeping* declared "stars made from gold and silver paper . . . made at home by little fingers that have little gold or silver. . . ." were fitting for the tree. But it was *Godey's Lady's Book* in December of 1880 that gave the most complete directions for making flat paper ornaments:

At the top of the tree, where the ornaments should be light, paper flowers, such as roses

*Pitchers, teapots, coffeepots, and chocolatepots were treasured items in the Victorian household and reproduced for the tree in both gold and silver patterned paper in addition to cotton and tinsel, all were trimmed with scraps, or embossed papers, 5³/₄"-6³/₄" h.*

and chrysanthemums, look well. Stars, hearts and other shapes cut from bright paper, and threaded on long strands of yellow or red wool, can be festooned among the branches with excellent effect.

The shapes such as stars, hearts, crescents, harps, anchors, axes and pitchers, although very simple, can be greatly varied. A pattern of each should be carefully cut in common stiff paper. If, for example, a star is cut in several tints, such as scarlet and blue, and pasted back to back, it can be strung upon the tree so as to show both sides as it swings. A small star in red pasted in the centre of a large star in yellow makes a gay effect, and these changes can be greatly varied by a little ingenuity. A harp made in green on one side and blue on the other, with strings of narrow strips of gold or silver, is pretty, and further alteration can be arranged by making the base of a contrasting color, or placing a little picture upon it. The pitcher can be greatly varied–a rim, handle and base can be made of a contrasting color, with a tiny star or picture on the side. The anchor is also susceptible of variation, the upper part being made to contrast with the lower.

A butterfly will repay the exercise of considerable ingenuity, but an easy way of producing a good effect is by simply cutting the entire shape out of one tint of paper and then cutting in the wings some small irregular holes or spots. Behind these, paper of a contrasting color can be placed, and then the same shape with varied punctures can be pasted beneath of another color. If the wings are then bent upwards to show both sides, it can be tied upon a twig, as if poised for flight. If several butterflies are shaped exactly in duplicate out of various colors, a neat effect can be produced by cutting them apart between the front and back, and pasting the two parts in contrasting colors together.

Stars and hearts of a variety of sizes can, however, be urged as producing the greatest show with the least expenditure of time and labor, as they can be pasted upon each other in a great variety of contrasting effects. A few half moons in silver or gold paper, threaded upon a string with such stars increases the variety of color. An axe with golden head and scarlet handle can be quite thrilling; the liberty bell and shield require more skill and patience. The chariot has been very much admired, with a body of gold upon crimson runners, and two small heads at the top to personate the happy occupants. . . .

All the patterns given have been quite successfully made by small children, and with a small supply of colored papers the little fingers can be soon taught to furnish an effect of bright decoration that cannot be equaled without a considerable expenditure in the gay trifles prepared by the toy-makers. If carefully taken care of, only a few additional novelties will be needed in subsequent years; but above and beyond all money valuation, will be found the store of fun for the fireside during the long December evenings, when old and young can exercise their ingenuity and taste in uniting in these pretty manufacturers, laying up a fund of bright memories to be recalled in after years, when the home circle may be perhaps dispersed forever.

*Shields, stars, and hearts are suggested as appropriate paper decorations for home manufacture in women's and children's popular literature from 1870-1890, 2⁷/₈″-7¹/₈″ h.*

Although paper ornaments were immensely popular during the last quarter of the nineteenth century and periodicals offered suggestions for making them, few patterns were printed. This reproduction from the 1880 December issue of Godey's is one and one-half times larger than the original, however it would still produce smaller ornaments than those found in antique collections.

When describing paper ornaments for home manufacture, the anchor, a symbol of hope, was always mentioned in women's magazines, $5^{1}/_{2}''$-$8^{5}/_{8}''$ h.

*Opposite page:*
*Ladies' legs and boots came out from under their skirts to become a popular motif for pincushions, cookie cutters, and glass slippers as well as tree ornaments, 2⁵/₅"-9¹/₂" h.*

*The old woman could keep many children in this black cardboard shoe, 13¹/₂" l.*

As stated earlier, creating the flat paper ornaments was, and is, a relatively simple process–tracing the pattern first on stiff backing then on fancy paper, cutting both shapes and pasting them together. Although mucilage, gum arabic or flour and water paste was originally used, for today's designer, rubber cement is advised since it easily rubs off where unwanted and does not cause the cardboard or fancy paper to curl or crinkle. Cardboard from the back of school tablets is the best weight but shoe boxes are also suitable. Foil wrapping paper with a small embossed design is the best substitute for gilt; one should avoid large patterns. The glazed paper is a shiny, solid-colored paper that for years was commonly used as shelf paper but is now available only in white. However, Hallmark and others have begun to feature shiny wrapping paper, the best source being "Crayon Colors" from the Stephen Lawrence Company listed in the appendix. Cellophane which was also used is commonly available during Easter and Christmas where fruit baskets are sold; Hallmark also offered red and green this past holiday season. Today's cellophane is not as stiff as the original but can be used with some degree of success. Although a short-cut method to ornament making is to use poster board which is already col-

*Nor is it necessary that much expense be entailed in the erection of a tree. Paper ornaments, (now the most fashionable) can be made of the most beautiful design, at trifling expense, if someone but about the house who has the 'bumps of construction' well developed . . .*

*Lancaster Evening Express,* December 28, 1875

ored, the effect is not as pleasing as covering the cardboard with the glazed paper. While the most detailed period suggestions for making the ornaments are found in *Godey's* December 1880 issue, the first step is omitted–that of cutting the cardboard and covering it–the method employed in *all* the antique ornaments studied. When selecting colors, remember that dark green is the least effective on the tree and that orange was seldom used. The most time-consuming activity is the trimming of the ornaments with strips of foil paper and scraps. Metallic fabric braid can be substituted, but it is not often seen on the originals. If this is desired, snap clothespins make excellent holders for the braid as it is drying. Old scraps can be found at flea markets, antique shops, or ordered by mail from Selfridges which is listed in the appendix. New scraps are available at Cost Plus outlets in California (no mail order), Christmas shops, stationery stores, and Brandon's Memorabilia, also listed in the appendix. Since gummed stickers on the market today have similar images but are not die cut, the use of delicate scissors to cut along outlines of the figures can remedy that situation. Patterns traced from the originals are included in the center section of the book and represent the spectrum of ornaments seen. Proportions of ornament sizes to trees was not a Victorian concern and should not be one today.

For variation, women used cotton batting or wadding, as it is sometimes called, to cover the flat paper shapes patterned after familiar household objects as well as forms like a star suspended in a circle or a multi-leaved clover (pp. 42, 43, and 44). Hand-sewn tinsel edged the shapes and marked divisions in the designs which were liberally sprinkled with stars, spangles, and scraps. Marguerite Hackenberg of Milton remembers that circa 1903 or 1904 her grandmother, Ida Kreitzer Haupt, cut out stars, crescents, sleighs and trolleys with windows, brushed them with glue she kept in a bottle, and pressed smooth cotton over the shapes. They were then trimmed by sewing "real fine tinsel" around the edge and dabbing little stars all over and some tiny colored pictures here and there. These charmingly described ornaments were

41

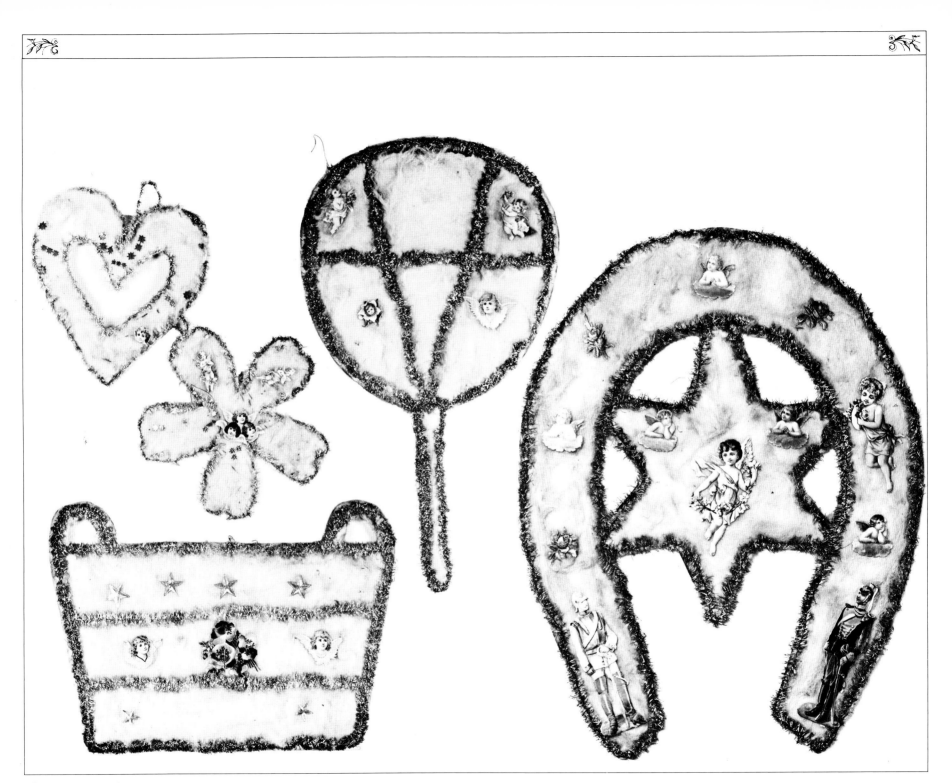

*Opposite page:*
*One informant recalls her grandmother cutting out cardboard shapes, covering them with cotton, and dabbing little stars on them, 7¹/₂"-17¹/₄" h.*

*Birds and bird cages were popular tree decorations, but this cotton-covered, tinsel-trimmed cage containing a white cockatoo and smaller exotic friends is perhaps one of the largest, 14¹/₂" h.*

handed-down to her mother, then to Marguerite and finally to her daughter, who, thinking them too tattered, disposed of them, a fate of many paper creations. One collector has a church with cellophane windows, two birds, an axe, and a key, in addition to a horse and wagon, a basket, and a canoe, all unfortunately discovered by the author too late to be included in the photography. Chester County Historical Society at West Chester has the largest public collection of these fluffy tree garnishes and displays them each year (pp. 8, 10, and 11).

Along with the cotton and tinsel ornaments, Chester County appoints their tree with homemade white and gold shapes (p. 46) similar to the popular machine-embossed and die-cut ornaments catalogued as flat Dresdens, although research by Malcolm Rogers has revealed that they were mainly produced in Berlin and environs. As with the other flat ornaments, shapes were traced on stiff white paper and on thin embossed gold and silver paper. After the two sheets were cut and glued together, there was little additional decoration applied; in the case of the pear, a leaf. Perhaps as a way to use the remaining scraps of the foil paper, purchased from a stationery store or saved from wrappings, small shapes like stockings were cut from the stiff white backing and stripes of gold foil were applied. As these homemade Dresdens twisted and turned in the candlelight they would give the tree as much fire as the manufactured ones. Dresden ornaments, advertised in this country by *Ehrich's Fashion Quarterly* in 1876, were priced by the dozen, seventy-five cents for the smallest; while the largest and finest were one dollar and sixty cents.

**P**aper, whether it was crepe, imported by Dennison in 1892 and later produced in this country by CA-Reed/Dennison, tissue, or glazed (flint), continued to be used for the tree decorations. *Godey's* (1880) describes two types of festoons for the tree which were later repeated by others. The first is the familiar chain:

The paper for this purpose should have the same tint on both sides; but a very handsome and stronger chain can be made fabricated out of the high-colored papers, that are tinted only on one side. For this take a strip of paper four inches in length and nearly one in width. Fold it sharply a little inwards from each edge, so as to make a narrow band entirely concealing the blank or untinted side of the paper. Touch one end of this band slightly with paste, and slip it neatly within the other end, pinch these ends firmly together, and a strong loop or link is finished. After folding the second band in the same manner, slip it through the first link before pasting, and they will be interlocked. Long links are more speedily prepared, but short links look better, and when made of crimson, deep blue or gold, they will well repay the labor expended, and can be preserved for use from year to year.

The second required folding and cutting, and the results were so pleasing it was highly recommended for ornamenting pictures and mirrors as well:

Most effective and easy of preparation are long paper chains, that can be fastened at the top of the tree, and allowed to drop in irregular festoons from branch to branch. A very simple chain is made by taking a long strip of paper, two and a-half inches in breadth, and doubling it sharply down the middle. Then cut alternately from each side of the strip, always taking care not to cut quite to the furthest edge of the strip. When the strip is unfolded, there will be seen a delicate chain of fragile loops.

In addition to these festoons, tissue paper was fringed and shaped as in the decorations given in *Demorest's* (1890):

Some of the showiest and least expensive of Christmas ornaments are the wreaths and angles of crimped tissue paper. They are made of inch-wide strips of tissue paper, finely fringed. Small wreaths to hang on the tree do not need to have the fringe curled; but to make large wreaths to hang on the wall, or festoons, etc., a fringe should be cut coarse and crimped with the scissors. Wind the fringed paper around the wire, keeping the fringe outside, and when a piece long enough is covered, twist the wire into the desired shape. The whole trunk of the tree is sometimes covered with similar strips of fringed paper.

*Opposite page:*
*Cotton batting and tinsel were favorite ornament materials for the women of the household, 2³/₄"-11¹/₂" h.*

*Robed in cotton trimmed with red crepe paper, the doll with jointed legs was commercially produced while her small companion appears to have been homemade from a paper doll pattern and a head from an advertisement, 7⁷/₈"-17¹/₂" h.*

narrow strip of white tissue-paper to its top point. Open the bag, slip the star inside, and suspend it half way from the top by pasting the end of the paper strip to the top of the bag. Make a loop of tissue-paper, fasten it to the top point of the bag, and then hang the snow pocket on the tree. The gold star gleaming through the frosty meshes is very pretty, but if you have several snow pockets there need not be stars in all. . . .

The crepe and tissue papers available at the turn of the century were also used to make flowers for the tree. *Godey's* and *Peterson's* like other household magazines printed a series about flower making with diagrams and directions for wax, feather, and paper blooms so lifelike they could not be distinguished from the real thing and obviously were longer lasting. The paper blossoms, "avowed ideal for the tops and tips of the branches where lightness mattered," were used on the tree. One article remarked that they should all be of one color, but the usual advice was to select tints and shades most like the natural specimen. *Godey's* earliest citation for a paper flower Christ-

mas ornament was 1862. The bell-flower was made from white paper cut in a rectangle, seven inches by eight inches. Both seven inch edges were cut into a fine fringe and curled over a thin pencil. The paper was then rolled into a tube with the fringe on the ends, glued, gathered in the middle and wound with white crochet thread to form two flowers. Three leaves should be added for the finishing touch. Roses, chrysanthemums and lilies were also

*Make a large crescent of pasteboard—thirteen inches from tip to tip is not too much—and after covering with the prettiest silver paper obtainable, hang it high up among the branches, so it will be seen to the best advantage.*

Harper's Bazar, 1887

By 1900 *The Delineator* not only repeated uses for the fringe but added a complex pattern for holly and berries which was the forerunner of the honeycomb drapes now enjoying revived popularity.

A variation on the festoon was a "pocket" from Lina Beard's "Christmas Decorations," which appeared in 1907:

The snow pocket is another pretty ornament and is made with a few snips of the scissors.

Cut a strip of white tissue-paper five and a half inches wide and twenty-two inches long. Fold the paper crosswise through the middle, then fold it again and again, until your folded piece is one inch wide. The folds must always be across the paper from start to finish. Now, cut slits in the folded paper, first a slit on one side, and then a slit on the other. Let the spaces between the slits be one eighth of an inch wide, and cut each slit to within one eighth of an inch of the edge. When this is done, carefully unfold the paper and spread it out flat, then lift the top edge with one hand, the bottom edge with the other, and gently pull the meshes apart. Gather the top edge into little plaits, and twist them together in a point; gather the bottom edge in the same way and twist that, then carefully pull the snow pocket out, and you will have a long, narrow bag of soft, white meshes. If it flares out too much, crush it together softly with your hand. Make a small, gilt paper star and fasten a

*Hand-cut from flat cardboard and covered with patterned gold and silver paper, these homemade decorations resemble the machine-cut and pressed shapes imported from Germany (Dresdens) which were popular from c. 1870-1920, 3¹/₂-8¹/₂" h.*

*Opposite page:*

*At the turn of the century, the Leiser family of Lewisburg was ornamenting the tree with paper stars, crescents, and pictures as well as small gifts. Courtesy: Martha and Robert Walgran.*

popular. Anna Garret of Chester County noted in her diary on December 19, 1885 that her sister took paper flowers to her teacher for a Christmas present and Anna was learning to make roses at home. ''The chrysanthemum ornament is showy and pretty, it is also very quickly made'' directed the *Delineator* in 1907, the last period directions for flower making studied:

Fold through the middle a piece of bright orange tissue-paper, six inches square. This will give you an oblong. Fold again through the middle crosswise, and you will have a smaller square. Bring the two opposite corners of the square together and fold, then cut off the point (side with cut edges) curving the edge, as if making a circle. The folded part of the triangle is at the diagonal, the edges at the bottom. Now cut slits in your triangle's edges (do not cut fold). Open it, and you will have a fringed circle. Make two fringed circles, lay one on top of the other, pinch the center in a point, twist it, and draw the fringed ends together. Make a writing-paper lamp-lighter for the stem, cover the point of the ornament with paste, insert it in the large end of the lighter, and press together with your fingers until it holds tight. In fastening the chrysanthemum ornament on the tree stand it upright and run a pin through the stem into one of the small branches. . . .

In addition to making flowers, another use of crepe paper was the covering of an ornament mentioned in *Godey's* in 1880. The article gave directions for rolling a piece of paper four inches by five around a staff shred of paper and fringing the ends. Although the article did not give further details, this is the size and shape of an ornament or party favor that has been used for over one hundred years, the cracker, snapper or motto. When the recipient pulled a tab on one end, there was a crack or snap as a cap makes when struck, and upon unwrapping, a prize was found in the center or a saying or motto, hence the variety of names. Offered for sale in most catalogs, they could be made for the components were also available. As the custom of putting them on the tree decreased, they gained in popularity as party favors and sad was the child whose motto didn't pop.

Although not as old a custom as the cracker, one paper furnishing for the tree presented in *Demorest's* (1890) which continued in popularity until the present generation is the paper lantern. From stories told by Union/Snyder citizens it was on everybody's tree:

The folding papers make cunning balloons, or lanterns, as they are sometimes called. Fold a paper in half, horizontally, and across this fold cut it in narrow strips to within half an inch of its open edges. Leave a half-inch margin on the sides. Open, and paste the sides together, so

*These flat cardboard animals covered with black glazed paper or gold foil appear to be cut and assembled by the same hand. Two horses and a pig were also seen in the same style, 1⁷/₈"-6" h.*

that you have a cylindrical shape, the strips running lengthwise. Add a strip of paper for a handle, and press the ends together so as to spread the strips out on the fold. These ends pushed close together, and fastened, spread the strips out in a wheel or rosette form, which would be nice for decorating purposes. When this ''balloon'' is made of a dark color, a gilt or silvered piece slipped inside makes it look bright. . . .

An additional paper embellishment that has enjoyed almost eighty years of popularity in the Union/Snyder area is the folded star (p. 50). Area newspapers published the directions and offered the paper strips, pale pink, yellow, blue, green and white, for pennies a package. Lillian Worrell Minnich (Milton resident) recalls buying paper in Sunbury in the 1920s at the corner of Center Street and Woodlawn Avenue and learning to make stars from her sister Edna who in turn had learned from an older sister, Arlene, born in 1902. Lillian said she made hundreds each year as they were never saved. The paper was also folded to form accordion-like icicles. Maude Engle, another area resident remembers that when her family moved to Shamokin in 1907 the local newspaper was publishing directions, and she said that some people out in the county near Shamokin only had stars on their trees. The stars were used to form crosses, baskets, and cradles, but no directions seem to exist for these shapes. William R. Rudolph, Glenbrook, Connecticut, patented the star pattern September 7, 1920, with directions so complex that the star would have been difficult to create. Mel-Co Printing of Sunbury have generously shared their pattern which was formerly printed in the *Sunbury Daily Item,* thereby preserving this Christmas tradition (p. 51):

How to Fold a Paper Star: to make a three-inch star cut accurately four strips of paper one-half inch wide and 17″ long. Use colored paper, plain, silver or gold or any colored Christmas wrappings. If the paper is colored on one side only, cut twice as wide and fold evenly down the length so that color is on both sides. Fold strips in middle as shown in fig. 1 and trim ends to form blunt points. Keep the points on the outside. Cut strips wider and longer to make larger stars.

According to Emily Lutz, a four-inch star requires 1 inch by 30 inch paper; one and one-fourth inch wide paper requires a strip eighteen and one-half inches long, a one and one-half inch wide strip requires a twenty inch length and a two inch wide strip requires a twenty-five inch strip in length. Quilling paper produces stars for a miniature tree.

*While it may be difficult to distinguish between some privately and commercially hand-made paper ornaments, these pink, gold, green, red, and blue shapes appear to be the outgrowth of juvenile imagination, 4¹/₂″-9¹/₂″ h.*

1. Place 4 folded strips in interlocking position to form a basket weave.

2. Tighten the basket weave until the four strips are firmly interlocked. Turn over. Holding in left hand, turn down front strip at upper left. Crease and turn star clockwise.

3. Turning paper clockwise, fold down three remaining top strips to form a second basket weave. When you turn down the fourth strip, weave it through the first strip as shown here.

4. Using short strips first, fold upper right strip away from you to make right angle triangle #1. Fold strip toward you to form triangle #2. Fold triangle #2 over #1 to form flat point as in fig. 5.

5. Weave end down through basket weave as shown. Turn clockwise and make points on three remaining upper right-hand strips. Push loose strip out of your way for last weaving.

6. Turn star over and repeat steps 4 and 5 until you have 8 points. Your star will then look like this . . . . four strips showing in back of four points and four strips covering four points.

7. To make center points take end of lower right-hand strip in right hand and with a loop motion, keeping right side up, push through upper lefthand basket weave and flat point.

8. Pull strip tight to form point. Turn star clockwise and continue until you have 4 points at center. Turn over and repeat on other side. Trim ends.

Note: You must fold strip #2, #3, and #4 out of the way to insert loops for points.

Dipping the stars in melted paraffin will make them waterproof for an outdoor tree, or keep them from crushing so that they can be used from year to year. Old stars were dipped in glue and then sprinkled with mica. To obtain a similar effect, the stars may be sprayed with glue and then dusted with diamond dust, a clear crystal-like substance available at craft stores.

The paper snowflake, another one of the area's long-time favorites, also did not appear in the national periodicals studied. It, too, was patented according to Malcolm Rogers on March 23, 1875 by William H. Backus of Boston, Massachusetts. It was not promoted as a trim for the tree, but as an educational toy consisting of a package of tinted papers with patterns for snow flakes printed on one-eighth of the page. When folded according to directions and cut on the lines indicated "paper flakes" resulted. The ubiquitous snow flake, the paper chain, and the lantern probably owe their existence to local school teachers.

Used on the tree in great abundance, paper also appeared occasionally under the tree, cut and pasted to form fences, houses, and barns for the Christmas villages (p. 52) which were an outgrowth of the putz tradition; a miniature reenactment of the manger scene in Bethlehem. The under-the-tree-scene might include circuses, log cabins in the woods, teepees and Indians, skating scenes on mirrored lakes, streams that ran or fountains that cascaded –only the time and talent of the creator limited the presentation. As one editor remarked:

A little garden or farm at the foot of the tree, such as has been described as fabricated out of paper, furnishes the children much amusement. . . . A house on a mossy mound with a few dolls, woolly sheep or chickens disposed on the declivity . . . while a fence cut like palings out of paper . . . will furnish to a child an amount of gratification utterly inexplicable to the grown-up mind.

Although ornaments of the same type as the ones just described, tinsel and scrap creations assembled in this country by firms such as Bernard Wilmsen's of Philadelphia and imported German Dresdens bedecked the tree, women were advised to add still more delights for the eye.

As early as 1876, *Ehrich's,* a New York toy store's catalogue, advertised gilded English walnuts for sale, twelve cents for a dozen, for the Christmas tree. At the turn of the century *Good Housekeeping* also advised using gilded English walnuts along with silvered chestnuts and bronzed pinecones. The housewife was instructed that before gilding the walnuts, she should carefully crack them, remove the kernels, and place a string between the halves before gluing them back together. The magazine also avowed that the silvered chestnuts were

*Patterns and paper for the folded star were sold by area newspapers as early as 1907 and some people recall joining the stars together to form such shapes as crosses and baskets, 2"-7" h.*

*Opposite page:*

*This photo attests to the popularity of the folded paper star in central Pennsylvania.*
*Courtesy: Fred G. Neece. Jr.*

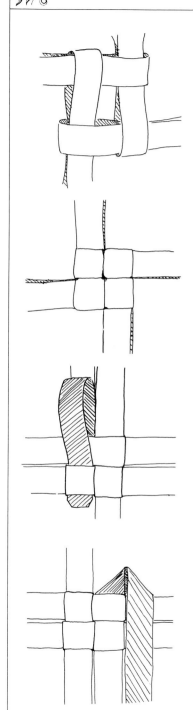

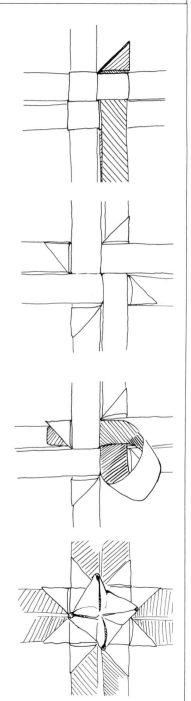

safe for the children to crack and eat after the tree was taken down. Strings of cranberries, peanuts wrapped in fringed paper, little men made from raisins or prunes strung together with needle and thread, and baskets for candy cut from orange peels were just a few things needed to make the tree replete. The periodicals were also crowded with suggestions for sewn, pasted, sawn, woven, beaded, knitted, and crocheted gifts to hang on the tree for uncles, aunts, cousins, and friends. Pin cushions, needle sharpeners, pen wipers, and shaving papers along with caps, music carriers, and map cases would have added more color to the branches. Of the one hundred-fifty gift suggestions offered by one magazine in the December issue, most were complicated, time-consuming but useful in the extreme, such as a chair fashioned from the breastbone of a duck, padded and used for a pin cushion!

The tree, once declared by an early German theologian to be a ''fiddle faddle, child's play not much better than mummeries and profanities, that tended to build Satan's chapel rather than God's church,'' finally received this accolade in the *Youth's Companion* of 1902:

The tree, brilliant with candles and tinsel, and bending under its load of gifts, has become so indispensable a part of our Christmas that we can hardly imagine a celebration of the festival

without it. We think of it as an immemorial institution. . . .

But among English-speaking people it has been so recently introduced that it may almost be called an innovation upon the historic Christmas. In England itself it was almost unknown before the middle of the last century, although English travellers had seen the pretty custom in German households and written much in praise of it. To America it came earlier, brought by German emigrants to Pennsylvania, and perhaps also by the Dutch settlers of New York.

But if the Christmas tree is, in a way of speaking, an exotic in England and America, it has certainly become thoroughly domesticated in both countries. Hardly an American household in which there are children, hardly a Sunday-school or an orphans' home but has its tree each year. Nearly if not quite five million little evergreens must be cut down this month to meet the demand. . . .

As long as we keep Christmas we shall want Christmas trees.


Christmas did enter hearts and homes across the country. It was embraced by women of many religious faiths and national backgrounds. Our American Christmas is a rich tapestry woven by these women with threads from their traditions. As long as they continue to endow the occasion with affection, hope, effort and care, there will always be Christmas.

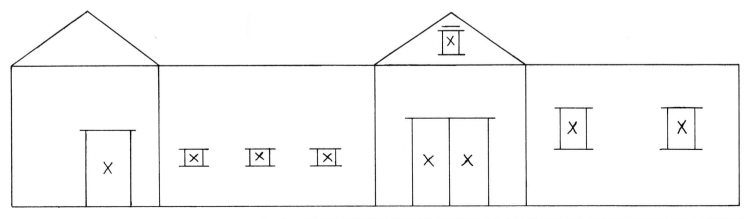

A star of immortelles centers the festoons of greens decorating the double parlors of the Sewell's home. Scrap pictures of snow children and angels in addition to paper dolls, flowers, and animals share the branches of this late nineteenth-century tree. Courtesy: Jim Morrison.

*The tree itself should be selected with care; a spruce or hemlock with the branches not too near together is best.*

Demorest's Monthly Magazine, 1887

Opposite page:
The putz, or miniature re-creation of the birth of Christ, developed into the Christmas tree yard which holds a paper barn and animals of papier-mache, wood, leather, or chalk. Courtesy: Carol and Jim Bohn.

This pattern for the body of a barn to be built of cardboard appeared in St. Nicholas, Vol. I, 1874. A rectangular piece served as a roof. It was part of a miniature putz called "Christmas City," in which the largest building was 2¹/₂" high.

ASTER, often referred to as the queen of days or queen of feasts, has a story, as Christmas does, that precedes the Christian festival. Just as Christmas is a meld of the pagan winter solstice with its greens and frolics and the Nativity, Easter is a blend of the celebration of the vernal equinox and the reaffirmation of eternity. The observance covers a three-month period beginning with Ash Wednesday, continuing through Lent, Holy Week, and Ascensiontide. It was associated with many folk beliefs such as Green Thursday, the "asherpuddle", and fastnachts, all of which are discussed in *Eastertide in Pennsylvania* (1960), a folkcultural study of Pennsylvania-Germans. The English, middle-Europeans, and Ukranians had their special customs which are detailed in *An Egg at Easter* (1971) by Venetia Newall. Two folk beliefs which won acceptance by most Americans were the decoration of the egg and the gift-giver, the Easter Bunny.

Similar to Christmas, the holiday receives very little notice in the press until the 1870s and then not as frequently as Christmas. For example, *Harper's* for the years 1850 through 1870 cited four entries for Easter while Christmas received twenty. One editor, Rev. W. C. Doane found it quite inexplicable that Easter never enjoyed the universal sentiment given to Christmas, for he said that if Christ had not risen, the baby born in December would have been just another child. Whether it was the increased German population in the country, a change of emphasis in the newspapers and periodicals, or the acceptance of Christmas in the 1870s, the late nineteenth century produced more Easter stories than any prior period. By 1875 the *Muncy Luminary* began devoting one to one and one-half columns to the festival at Saint James, although they noted the celebrations had been occurring for many years. The *Lewisburg Chronicle* introduces its sporadic coverage over the next few decades with the terse comment on April 19, 1867, "Today is Good Friday, consequently next Sunday is Easter." By 1910 Rev. Doane reported that some great Protestant churches, who used to ignore the holiday, were keeping it quite as much as the Catholics and Episcopalians; it had also always been kept by the "gay" Dutch: the Moravians, the Lutherans, and the Reformeds.

In many ways the celebration of Easter paralleled that of Christmas; both had gift givers, both had receptacles for the gifts, both were finally accepted by Protestant faiths, in addition to depending on the housewife to make the preparations. As the holidays developed, the tree became the symbol of Christmas while the egg became the focus of Easter. Craft columns in the ladies' periodicals gave almost as many ways to decorate the egg as the tree and were similarly helpful with ideas for the adornment of the church and a few guides for the home for Easter, primarily party suggestions.

As Christmas had its gift-giver that traveled to bring presents, Easter had the bunny, whose origin is as shadowy as that of Santa Claus. One delightful tale is about a medieval princess, who wishing to anonymously thank her people, went about placing colored eggs in nests throughout the countryside. Children discovered the treasures, and while exclaiming about the surprise, saw a rabbit run out from under one of the bushes and thought he had left the gifts.

In the same way that Santa knew, the rabbit seemed to know who had been good and who had not, for Willis Hause remembers one Easter vividly. His father was very strict, particularly about strong language, and the boys knew the consequences of using it. Therefore, he was quite surprised one Easter morning to be awakened by a loud curse from his brother damning the bunny. Upon closer inspection, it appeared the rabbit had filled his brother's cap with pellets instead of eggs.

Although the bunny was readily accepted in Germany and among the German immigrants from the upper Rhine, Switzerland, and the Palatinate, he was unknown in other parts of middle-Europe and England as well as the United States before advertising exploitation. Two senior residents of Union County, the Ralph Adamses moved from Massachusetts as young adults and were amazed to find the bunny living in Pennsylvania, but espoused the belief for the sake of their children. In contrast, Pennsylvania-German Marie Foust always knew there were two kinds of eggs–white ones the chicken laid and brown ones the bunny laid. The brown eggs that the bunny laid were dyed by the housewife by boiling them with onion skins (p. 64) and appeared as gifts on Easter morning in nests made by the children with grass or as Hazel Burrey did by cutting last year's sales bills into slender strips. Eggs also appeared in plates or dishes such as the Dieffenderfer children would select from among their mother's best ones, or in caps like William Conrad's, which was probably the most common practice. A few children in Union County had high-handled baskets which they used each year for Easter.

This giving of eggs on Easter was not a practice that originated in Germany or was confined to Christians, for Venetia Newall gives examples of Hindu, Mohammedan, and Jewish customs. Some of the most beautifully decorated eggs in this country are those done by Lithuanian, Ukranian, and Polish Americans (p. 60).

*While her mother is away, Madge is teaching Bessie to color eggs for gifts in this March 31, 1888 illustration from* Golden Days. *Courtesy: Library of Congress.*

*The giving of an egg as a mark of friendship or love is almost as old as the ark, of which it is a symbol; for the ancients used it as a sign of resurrection, and brought eggs to the altars for their gods as gifts . . .*

Harper's Young People, April 12, 1881

This 1878 illustration in a popular children's periodical, Saint Nicholas, *helped promote the German tradition of the egg-laying rabbit.*

Oral tradition and research credit the women with the responsibility for the decoration of the egg. In middle-European countries it was a token of love, and the suitor could tell his standing in his young lady's estimation by the number of eggs he received. In Bohemia a gift of two was often accompanied with this verse:

> You old ass,
> Stay at Home.
> I give to you two eggs,
> Love is gone.

However the astute lover knew that even if he received twelve eggs "it was a long way from eggs to marriage." In Lithuania only single girls decorated the eggs, and only on Easter afternoon, while in Poland girls did them during Lent. Skilled older women in the village might be hired by a girl if she felt her eggs would not please her suitor. Designs, a guarded secret, were a source of family pride.

In Pennsylvania both sexes participated in the egg decorating whether using wax-resist or carving. Alfred Shoemaker cites few women carvers; however, many of his descriptions refer to professional egg-scratchers who were working mostly in the last quarter of the nineteenth century and were retired from occupations that had required manual dexterity like

tailoring, cobbling, or engraving. Although presentation eggs were not a custom in Union/Snyder counties, some were made. In 1925 according to John Charles Rousch, there was a German immigrant tailor, Jake Freese, who scratched eggs in the Selinsgrove area. More common were the eggs described by Mary Kocher Bogar and Olive Thompson Hoover. Their mothers, grandmothers, and aunts used to scratch their names and a "peep," bunny, or flower on the familiar onion-skin dyed egg. While the egg was still warm, they would wipe it with a bit of lard and polish it until it was shiny. When asked how her mother did it, Olive replied that she just took an old kitchen fork with a broken tine and scratched. "She was the only one about who seemed to do it." Mrs. Thompson was not the only woman to do it in Pennsylvania for in the collection at the Historical Society of York County are six eggs carved by Susan Smyser who chose flowers and animals for her themes (p. 57). The Historical Society of Berks County has three eggs donated by Matilde W. Otto presumably done by C. (Clara) B. F. who also chose flowers. A private collector near Reading has a presentation egg from Kate B. Lotz to Emma B. Hafer done on Monday, April 22, 1878 and inscribed with purple drawings of a house, pigs (marked sow), a rider on a horse, a man and a rider in a cart, indicating that the sex of the scribe cannot be determined by the imagery. Shoemaker in *The Pennsylvania Dutchman* (1955) mentioned an egg marked *Bessie's gift from Mama April 18, 1890* as well as an earlier egg dedicated *Mama and Papa's gift to their baby, our Bessie; Columbia, April 25, 1886,* suggesting that Mama could have done both eggs.

If women did not carve all the eggs, they did inspire some of the presenters; M. W. O., Emma Locke, Emma Hafer, Lizzie, Jennie Lint, Mary E. Witmer, Catharine Schmuker, and Bertha Cochran received them as well as an anonymous *grat gramma.* Possibly the oldest decorated egg, wax resist not scratch-carved as reported, is one received by a woman marked *M. B. 1774.* Now in the Pennsylvania Folklife collection, it could be the same egg reported in the Mount Joy *Herald* (1880s) by

Jacob N. Brubaker as formerly belonging to Mara Brubaker.

In addition to suggestions for decorating the eggs, periodicals such as *The Youth's Companion* and local newspapers such as the *Muncy Luminary* detailed the adornment of the churches by women's committees. Arches of roses and smilax with festoons of greens marked the architectural features of one church while the back of the altar was banked with greens and at each end was a bouquet of flowers. "High above the altar was the motto, 'Christ is Risen,' fashioned more tastefully than ever." All the church windows were filled with growing plants and the organ was beautifully trimmed with vines and flowers. The chancel steps were bordered with flowers and on the altar was a large floral cross. Directions for making similar crosses for the home or the church were offered in *Our Homes and How to Beautify Them* (1888):

The cross, which is inappropriate at Christmas, is largely used as an Easter emblem, covered with flowers. . . . The frame, made of any kind of wood, no matter how rough, is 12 to 14 inches high, and the length of the arms in proportion. Gather from the woods a large quantity of the soft crinkly moss which clings to rocks in damp places, and carefully dry it in the sun for a few hours, then scrape off the loose earth. Make a stiff paste of flour and water, and spread it over the back of the moss, and cover the entire cross. Paste a piece of scarlet flannel on the bottom to keep the table from being scratched. While collecting the moss, gather also other ornamental things, such as the little red cups and white cups among the gray lichens and little twigs covered with them. The Bittersweet is another essential ornament. Tiny autumn leaves and small ferns can be pressed and made of great service. When the moss covering is dry, the cross is ready for decorating. Beginning at the base, make a mound all around it of the little red and white cups; stand among these the little moss-covered twigs, also ferns, and a delicate variety of dried grasses. The body of the cross may be arranged according to taste, adding the different kinds of mosses and lichens, which grow on rocks in various shapes and colors. A small vine that nature has gayly colored may be pressed, and gracefully twined across the front. Add the Bitter-sweet berries to help give brilliance. A few natural flowers, or

artificial ones of paper or wax, add greatly to its beauty. When the decorating is finished, drape in a light, graceful manner with hanging masses of light moss. . . .

Decorations for the home focused on stands for the eggs or party decorations for holiday luncheons and children's festivities. Containers for the eggs which were served for breakfast might have been baskets made from pasteboard or stands made from wire or twigs, looking very much like bird baths or if fashioned for table tops, miniature ones.

For commemorating Easter, *Good Housekeeping* suggested luncheons with floral themes in 1901. For a lily party, not only did the table have bouquets of lilies in the center, with small bouquets of lilies of the valley on each napkin and cardboard place tags made to resemble lilies, but also the food was green and white, consisting of cream soup, chicken salad, celery, and pistachio ice cream in the shape of a lily with white grapes. Fortunately the violet luncheon plans concerned only the table appointments. It was suggested that Easter breakfast might be planned using the yellow jonquil for a centerpiece and eggs for the main course. Saffron-tinted bread, butter, yellow-tomato preserves and yellow table linens would complete the theme. Another meal-time suggestion

and decoration, as well, necessitated breaking egg shells carefully at the tip, using only a small opening, then emptying the egg shells, washing them carefully, and letting them dry in a container that would hold the shells upright. One then prepared blancmange (cornstarch-type pudding), dividing it into as many dishes as colors were desired; tinted the pudding and poured it into the egg shells to harden. A jelly was made using lemon juice and gelatin that had been colored with saffron. When the jelly was firm, it was cut into irregular pieces. At serving time grandmother's three-tiered dish or March stand was lined with this gelatin, the blancmange eggs were unpeeled and placed on the jelly and served to each guest with candied peel made from the rinds of the lemons. This recipe of the editor's grandmother was published by *Good Housekeeping's* food editor in 1901. The same idea was used traditionally by one family, except that the eggs were filled with fruit gelatin and were nested in the parsley surrounding the baked ham on the Easter table. (For additional suggestions for table settings consult a recent Winterthur publication, *The Festive Tradition: American Table Decorations and Desserts, 1670-1900* by Louise C. Belden, 1983.)

The ubiquitous egg not only was the main stay of Easter breakfast (there are stories of people eating as many as twelve); it decorated the tables and provided the craft material for gifts for the occasion: tea sets (p. 63), pen wipers, shaving papers, sachets, and plant holders as Mrs. C. S. Jones directed in *Household Elegancies* (1875):

Open a hen, duck, or goose egg at the pointed end; let all the contents run out, and cut the upper, smaller half away with small sharp scissors; fill it almost up with earth, and plant a sedum, which, despite the small space, thrives splendidly and spreads out its little twigs on every side. As outer decoration for this improvised flower-pot, a net-work of crochet suspended by cord made of chain-stitches, and trimmed with tassels, will do nicely.

*Cassell's Household Guide* which was printed in London and New York made these additional suggestions:

Another way of making Easter eggs is to boil them very hard; cut each egg in half; remove the meat. Gum a piece of silk, satin, or ribbon, with the top drawn up previously like a bag, with a frill of strings, and put a strip of prettily-embossed gold paper over the join of the silk and the egg. Fill the egg-bag with sweetmeats, or any little present you wish to make–such as a ring or a thimble, laid at the top of sugarplums. Eggs dyed may be cut in half, and then scratched prettily; the meat afterwards removed, and a bag added. . . .

Another way of making an Easter egg is to boil one very hard. Cut it in half lengthways; bind the edge of each half with gold paper; gum a ribbon across the hollow of each, leaving ends at both sides. Sew two ends together, in a bow, to make a hinge; fill the egg with sweetmeats, or some little gift, and, having closed it, tie the ribbon-ends.

Anyone attempting to copy the directions offered in the early periodicals should heed the advice of one editor who suggested soaking the shells in warm water before cutting them into shapes. Grace DeHart, an egger from Middletown, confirms that this practice is applicable today; overnight is not too long.

One use of the egg shell, decorating indoor egg trees, was not discussed in the newspapers or periodicals studied, although authors Daniel Lord and Alfred Shoemaker quoted a description of a tree from *Lothrop's Annual* (1895). Shoemaker also reported the appearance of the indoor decorated-egg tree at the homes of John McQuate of Denver, Clyde Artman of Yeagertown, and Carrie M. (Mrs. Elmer) Palsgrove of

*According to Mifflinburg resident William Conrad, setting his cap on Easter Eve for many years provided a nest for the Easter bunny to fill, 6¹/₂" h.*

Reading in the 1920s. Carrie Palsgrove was known to have decorated a tree for twenty-five years, and it was during this time that Cornelius Weygandt became acquainted with the custom which he described in *The Blue Hills* (1936). Weygandt also was said to be responsible for introducing author Katherine Milhouse to Carrie Palsgrove, and it was Carrie's tree that inspired Katherine Milhouse's 1950 award-winning children's book which helped to further popularize the custom of decorating egg trees in America. The tree's origin may never be known. Shoemaker suggested that popular German-printed postcards picturing the tree were a possible origin. However, of the ten thousand Easter postcards collected by Grace DeHart of Middletown only four exhibited pictures of an egg tree; one was postmarked 1907. Venetia Newall described the early European folk use of the decorated-egg tree both as a celebration of the death of winter and a rite of courtship. She postulated that the close proximity of spring celebrations and Easter with its moveable date had helped to blend the customs, obscuring the origin. Whatever its beginning the decorated-egg tree has become an Easter tradition.

Articles in the 1880s discuss primarily the dyeing and decoration of the egg. Eggs could be colored by boiling them with leaves and roots found around the home (p. 64). Onion skins or peelings gave yellow when the egg was quickly removed from the water and reddish-brown or burnt sienna when left longer in the decoction; spinach leaves produced green, walnut hulls, burnt umber, and the saffron bed (a necessity for Pennsylvania-German housewives) yielded yellow. Also, Maude Engle reported that the sassafras root gave pink. There were other vegetable dyes available at the drug store: logwood, cochineal, cudbear, and annatto. The logwood, a bark from a tropical American tree of the pea family, appeared to be the most versatile for depending on the addition of a mordant it could

produce violet, red, or blue. Cochineal made from a tropical beetle yielded red; cudbear from lichens, violet; and annatto from the waxy substance around the flower of a tropical plant, red-orange. The aniline dyes from coal tar were said to be more reliable, but were not favored by many for they were thought to be poisonous. This bias continued in central Pennsylvania for many informants said their mothers refused to buy the dyes packaged in paper and used onion skins or catkins from an alder (allehecka). In contrast, Laura Walter was quite proud that her father ran a store and they always had store-dyed eggs–the favorite was purple.

Eggs could be decorated before or after they were dyed. The wax-resist method was used for designing the egg before it was dyed. Early directions were found in *Saint Nicholas* (1875), *Golden Days* (1888), and *Our Homes* (1888):

If you would like to have names or mottoes written on the shells dip a brush or a new quill pen in melted white wax; trace whatever words or design you choose, then put it on to boil; that the other part of the egg will receive any dye in which it is emerged, the tracery will remain white and legible.

To simply color the eggs, they need only be dipped in water, then placed in a decoction of logwood for the various shades of purple, of cochineal for red, or boiled with onion peelings, or in an onion, for amber, or colored with spinach-juice for green. But superior to these simple colorings are aniline dyes, which may be obtained of any color, and can be used as paints on shells as well as dyes.

*Easter-Monday is the proper time for the presentation of peace eggs, and to prepare them is always a work of love; . . .*

Harper's Young People,
April 12, 1881

The eggs are dipped in water before being put in the dye, to make them take the color evenly. If it is desired to keep part of the shell white–for instance, to have a name or motto in white on a red ground, proceed thus:

When the egg is warm, after boiling, take a small piece of mutton suet, which, being hard, you can cut to a point almost like a pencil. With this, draw or write what you wish on the warm egg, which you can then place in the dye.

The part greased will not take the color, but when dry the fat is easily removed, and the white design can be left or filled in with another color, or with a little gold or silver paint.

Another way is to dip the egg into hot water, and then write a name or motto on the shell with tallow. It is then boiled in the solution of dyewood, when the inscription will appear in white, upon a colored ground.

Cornelius Weygandt described the wax-resist decoration of eggs in *The Blue Hills* (1936). Many of the eggs he discussed can be seen at the Philadelphia Museum of Art. Most contacts in Union/Snyder counties remembered drawing on the egg with wax before dyeing as their families' way of decoration. Many immigrants from middle-Europe continue to use the method, but employ a pin and heated beeswax to produce the eggs known as krashanky (singular krashanka). Sometimes a two-color design is produced by making comma-like lines of wax on the dyed egg in the same manner as they were made on the white egg, then dipping the egg in a second color. Krashanky were meant to be eaten.

Another form of the wax-resist decorated eggs known as pysanka (plural pysanky, pysanki) was not intended for eating, but for presentation, often by a girl to her boy-friend. Also, a basket of these eggs was kept in the home as protection against fires and lightning. Requiring as many as five hours of work and a steady hand, the dyeing process is described in several books in the bibliography. Basically, a raw egg is dipped into a series of cold dyes, progressing from the lightest to the darkest–green and blue being applied by hand for they tend to "muddy" the other colors. After each dipping, the portion of the egg which is to remain that color is covered with hot beeswax applied by a pin, a needle or a writing tool called a kitska which was specifically designed for the art. When all dyes are dry and the design completed, the egg is warmed and the wax removed. Since a full egg can explode and negate the time and talent devoted to the task, many recent eggs are blown after the pattern is accomplished.

The colors and the shapes on the egg are significant; many being transmitted by families or related to geographical areas. Red is said to denote love; blue, health; green, money; and orange, attraction. The geometric, plant, and animal designs also have their own meaning. The dot or small circle is said to represent stars; the belt or ribbon, eternity; the triangle or diamond shaded with cross lines is the trinity, three stages of man, or fire, air and water; ladders divide the patterns. The rose, often indistinguishable from the star–except that the rose almost always appears as the center motif on the side of the egg–is thought to be the sun while the pine tree symbolizes eternal youth and health. Animal images seen are ram's horns, bird's feet, butterflies, spiders, as well as hens which symbolize fertility or achievement of wishes; fish, Christianity; and reindeer, wealth and prosperity. Some Ukranians, the Hutzuls, believe that as long as people decorate pysanky, the world will continue to exist.

A third form of decorated eggs done by Ukranians is the driapanky or scratched egg. It is probably the oldest form of decorating according to Wasyl O. Luciw and George Wnnysky in *Pennsylvania Folklife* (1972). Photos accompanying their article show the work of Diana Tyma who does the eggs in the manner which her grandfather

*For Easter, the pysanka or wax resist egg was created by families of Polish, Lithuanian, and Ukraninan descent using traditional regional patterns, 2"-2¹/₂" h.*

taught her, geometric designs divided by ladder-like lines, scratched after the raw egg had been dipped in a single color dye. In contrast, Annie Morgalis, a third-generation Lithuanian egg-carver, cooks her eggs before scratching them and uses both geometric and naturalistic images. According to Venetia Newall in *An Egg at Easter* (1971), the scratching is practiced by Mennonites in Pfalz, as well as East Prussians, Lausitzans, Lithuanians, Slovenians, Czecks, Bohemians, Silesians, and Slovakians. The last four acquired the skills in

the nineteenth century. For further information about customs and techniques as well as colors and designs, consult the bibliography for books by Evelyn Coskey, Anne Mitz, and Venetia Newall.

Other countries used scratch-carving to decorate eggs. Venetia Newall and Winnifred Cunningham describe the English technique, mostly disappeared, which is demonstrated by the collection of eggs scratched in the years 1868-1878 and displayed at the Wordsworth Museum in Cumberland, England. The eggs

were systematically divided into three areas and then scratched with the date, the recipients's name, and swans, landscapes, birds or flowers. Eggs with cupids were a speciality of schoolboys for Valentine's Day. The red-brown color from onion-skins was used most frequently, but red and black were also popular.

Newall and Shoemaker cite the same references for dating the Pennsylvania-German scratching technique–Thomas Anburey's *Travels Through the Interior Parts of America* (1789) and a Moravian letter which mentioned "old folks scratching tulips" in 1829. Similar to middle-Europeans who borrowed their egg designs from their embroidery, pottery, and wall decorations, the Pennsylvania-Germans might be expected to use the same motifs on their eggs as their fraktur, pottery, punch-decorated tinware, and blanket chests. To a limited extent they do; stylized flowers in an urn, tulips, hearts, and birds are repeated on some of the scratch-carved eggs. Two eggs in the Lancaster County Historical Society collection marked *ESH/1869* and *FEH/1872* (p. 58) and one in a private collection in Lancaster engraved *Edgar H. Herr/1869* have the traditional urn with abstract flowers. The *Herr/1869* egg is pictured in *The Pennsylvania Dutchman* (1955) in an article by Alfred Shoemaker who noted that it was one of a collection which he knew was purchased at the same place, although the other eggs from the collection had distinctly different imagery. In the collection of The Historical Society of Berks County is an egg engraved *Clara /1857*, and in the Schwenkfelder Museum at Pennsburg is one inscribed *Thomas K. Shultz April 17, 1870*, both exhibiting an urn and flowers; another one scratched *ALG/1894* is in the Pennsylvania Folklife collection. Other traditional urns and flowers appear in private collections inscribed *EHD/1876, AW/1869, SEG/1880,* and one undated example; all but two of the eggs were traditionally colored with onion skins. One exception *FEH/ 1872* was dyed purple and the other *Shultz/1870* was black. A well-executed tulip appeared on an egg dated *1818* at the Schwenkfelder Museum as well as on several in the Pennsylvania Folklife collection.

Even though eggs were thought to be tokens of love, the heart, which is frequently found on Pennsylvania-German pieces, was seen but once in the public and private collections viewed (p. 64). It was scratched into a hen's egg dyed traditionally with onion skins. The heart also appeared on Lizzie Cammauf's 1888 egg illustrated in *The Pennsylvania Dutchman* (1955).

If the heart is used infrequently, the bird is not. The typical Pennsylvania-German stylized bird or distelfink is found on eggs in the Pennsylvania Folklife collection, now housed at Ursinus College. They are some of the strongest designs but unfortunately the eggs require restoration. Done by a sure hand, they seem to have been commissioned for the scratcher left a blank cartouche on four of the twelve eggs. In this series at Ursinus, some seem to have been done for a family with the last initial *G* for they appear in this order: *HLG/1883, ALG/1889, CLG/1889, CLG/1893, ALG/1894,* and *ALG/1904.* The remaining initialed eggs were marked *SAL/1865* and *MAL/1897;* all were shades of red-violet.

An image that is treated in both a stylistic and naturalistic manner is the flag. Sometimes it is shown flying, sometimes straight, and at other times it is incorporated into a shield with stars across the top and stripes down the length of the shape. Just as patriotism was evident on the tree, it is seen on the eggs, for Liberty and the eagle were scratched on one vivid red-violet egg (p. 59).

Religious iconography was present on two eggs. One in a public collection at the Schwenkfelder Museum was marked with the cross and anchor, a symbol of hope, and was inscribed *M S Krauss/March 29, 1880;* The second, in a private collection, was inscribed with a cross, *Julia A. Gilgore, I(J) Asbury Gilgore, Easter Joys, 1890.* Much has been written about the meaning of the Pennsylvania-German images; the ark or boat on two eggs could have biblical connotations as well as the fish seen on several. However, the majority of the images appear to represent farm implements and ordinary barnyard animals, not religious symbols.

In contrast to the stylized drawing of objects, there is realistic or naturalistic drawing on some of the eggs. Birds are frequently scratched in a naturalistic manner or at least in an attempt to copy nature. They appear in combination with the urns and rural scenes. The Historical Society of Berks County possesses an egg with a strikingly well-executed bird and the name and date *"MPMiller/1860"* as well as a less bold peacock-like creature on a blue egg marked *Jennie 1873.* In private collections were a fine-lined peacock on a stump (p. 58) and a flying dove (p. 64) as well as the quails of B. Elmer Leaman (p. 64). When purchased at a sale in Ephrata, the two *BEL* eggs were accompanied by a clipping which credited them to B. Elmer Leaman, a Bird-in-Hand Justice of the Peace who was known to have carved eggs with a penknife for almost sixty years until he could no longer see. According to Lancaster historian Elizabeth Clarke Kieffer, Leaman died February 6, 1948, making the *1946* egg one of his last, unusual for the multicolor washes used as a background.

Naturalistic flowers appear on several of the eggs found in The Historical Societies of Berks and York Counties. In Berks the *MWO/186(?)* egg has four sprays of flowers, one being a rose, deeply carved into a black background, while the *MPMiller/1860* egg has a cluster of flowers deftly but lightly scratched on one end of the onion-skin dyed egg. The floral eggs in York were the gift of Jennie E. Lint in 1939. At that time she said the six eggs were done by Susan (Mrs. John) Smyser with the penknife that was included with the basket of eggs. Susan Smyser (b.1817-d.1908) lived at 327 West Market from 1904-1907 according to directories researched by Pat Tomes. This was also the address given for Annie Lint, sister to Jennie, and Jennie herself after 1925. The exact relationship of Susan Smyser to the Lints is not known although an Elizabeth Smyser was their maternal grandmother. We do know that Susan's carefully scratch-carved eggs made in 1883, 1884, 1885, 1886 and 1888 were treasured by Jennie for fifty-one years before being entrusted to the museum. On one egg with birds and a bouquet of flowers, the 1880 date is not clearly executed and could be interpreted as 1884 or 1887. The other egg dated *1884* had perhaps the most realistic portrayal of flowers; the calla lily, lily of the valley, and pansy are readily identified (p. 57).

Not only did Susan draw her birds and flowers in a realistic manner, but the cat is remarkable; the carving includes the rendering of individual hairs. This egg has *age 66* inscribed which would appear to be the age of Susan Smyser rather than that of Jennie E. Lint. Easter is not mentioned on any of the exquisite

*Decorated with the pith of the great bulrush, Juncus effusus, and scraps of calico, the two eggs on the left are the work of Laura Huyett, a one-time student of Viola Miller who made the others, 2″ – 3¹/2″ h.*

*Paper-dressed candy containers from the 1897 April* Demorest's. *Courtesy: Library of Congress.*

eggs, but the bunnies, bugs, and butterflies portrayed by the engraver are spring-like. The significance of the clock with its hands noting five after seven on the "1888" egg is unknown.

In addition to the clock face drawn by Susan Smyser, one other was seen. It was a face of a tall case clock carved into a onion-skin dyed turkey egg owned by The Historical Society of Montgomery County. Dated *1832,* the egg presents a panoply of images: a flowering bulb, a realistic coiled snake, a wine glass, a decanter, a turtle, in addition to the tall case clock and a lady in a sunbonnet.

Full figures as seen on the Montgomery County egg are rarely found drawn in a naturalistic manner; most scratchers draw stick-like people. A turkey egg in a private collection marked with the date *1826* has a man with a cane, a lady with a bouquet as well as a tree, and one in the public collection of the Philadelphia Museum of Art shows a soldier returning home, a hoop-skirted lady greeting him, and is inscribed *Mary E. Whitmer, 1865. Dear Cousin do not forget me.* This egg also features a house, a barn, a tree, a flagpole and a flag!

Houses, barns and trees appear with some regularity (pp. 58 and 64). In public collections the *Whitmer/1865* egg described before and an *1891* egg in the Pennsylvania Folklife collection at Ursinus College have such imagery. A building which appears less frequently than the barn or the house is the church. Two examples can be viewed in public collections: one in the Pennsylvania Folklife collection marked *CLG/ 1889* and another at The Historical Society of York County inscribed *Florrie/1860* (p. 65). On the reverse of this egg is a tower on a hill with a flag, giving the impression of a monument. Although not a building but a structure, the ark or sailing boat is seen also (p. 64). The artist often draws a sun or moon and stars above the buildings; however on the *MWO/ CBF* egg donated by Maltilde W. Otto to The Historical Society of Berks County, the crescent moon and stars are used alone.

In addition to the stylized eggs with some typical Pennsylvania-German designs and the naturalistically-drawn eggs are eggs with geometric patterns. The patterns, used by Polish, Lithuanian and Ukranian egg decorators to cover the entire egg, appear more regularly only on the ends of the Pennsylvania-German carved eggs (p. 58). The top and bottom of the eggs were engraved with stars, crosses, or concentric rings, sometimes incorporating dates, names, and locations. The eggs designated previously as belonging to the *Herr/1869* collection illustrate this as well as eight purchased by Triplett Antiques at a Taneytown, Maryland sale.

Some examples of eggs with overall geometric decoration are: one covered with stars and crosses on a yellow-brown onion-skin dyed egg; one with horizontal lines inscribed *April 17, 1881 Lillie M. Wilson Lincon* on the traditional dark red-brown background; and a checkered example on a purple-brown onionskin dyed background, engraved *Cyrus W. April 5, 1871* (pp. 58 and 59). Scratch-carved eggs with overall patterns of stylized stars can be seen at the Philadelphia Museum of Art; both are onion-skin colored.

Eggs which are more noteworthy for their dates than for their designs can be seen at the Schwenkfelder Museum, *SK/1808;* The Historical Society of Berks County, *Joseph Hiester 1813;* the Lititz Historical Foundation, *JG/ BC(G)/1822,* and *When Howard We Thee Aw-y/1835,* and the Philadelphia Museum of Art, *April 10, 1841.* Since Shoemaker recounts stories of people receiving eggs with birthday dates, it cannot be assumed that all years on eggs signify the date decorated.

Eggs are more conventionally divided horizontally into three sections: top, middle, and bottom (p. 64). Some of the eggs seen, however, were divided vertically into six or eight sections like the presentation egg of *J. R. Thoman for Mae Wolf,* a music teacher in *East Berlin* on *March 29, 1891* (p. 59). Shoemaker pictures a similarly designed egg in *The Pennsylvania Dutchman* (1955) and one in the collection of The Historical Society of Berks County is scratched *JAD, grat gramma, March 31, 1907.*

Most eggs were boiled in a dye bath producing a solid-colored egg which was then deco-

rated by scratching or scratch-carving through the color to the white shell. The dye on some eggs was atypical (pp. 58-59); the first in a private collection dated *March 29, 1891,* the other dated 1875 on display at the Lancaster County Historical Society. Both of these eggs were colored by dabbing or blotting dye on a very hot egg so that the dye would dry in blotches, appearing mottled. On these two eggs only a date was carved in fine Spencerian handwriting. Two other eggs exhibited unusual coloring: the Leaman eggs. They were painted with dyes, producing multicolored backgrounds of brown, green and purple.

Overall styles of the eggs differ greatly in part dictated by the skill of the draftsman. Scratchers like Smyser and Leaman are profes-

*Using the pattern that appeared in the April 1895 issue of Demorest's at right, one could make a tea service as below, 2³/₄" h., by simply tracing patterns onto white cardboard, cutting and then pasting them to cut egg shells.*

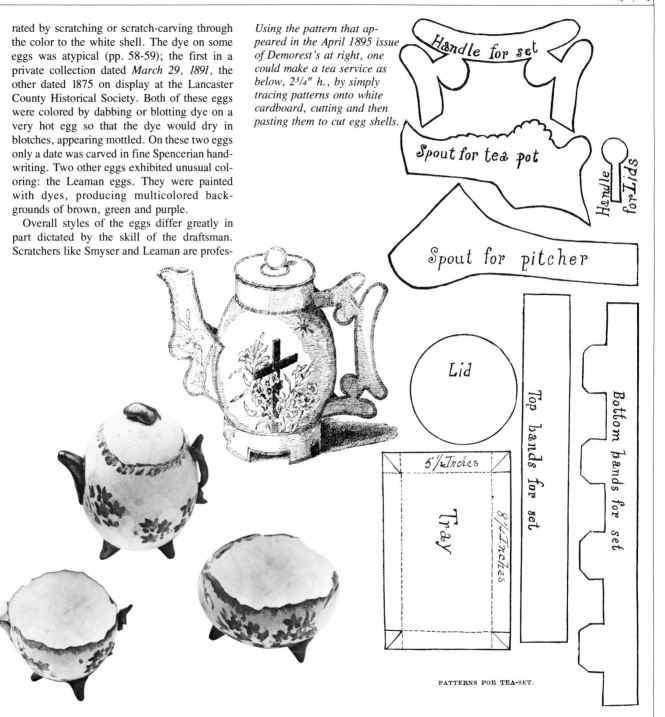

PATTERNS FOR TEA-SET.

63

*Surrounding this circa 1904–1906 H. Winslow Fegley photograph from the Schwenkfelder Library in Pennsburg, Pennsylvania are examples of scratch-carved Easter eggs. Lower left to right: Two eggs represent the work of B. Elmer Leaman who carved more than two hundred painted eggs each year on commission. The reverse of the 1869 egg has a tree, a house, and a potted plant; the 1896 egg contains a tree, another bird, a dog,* Lancaster, Pa, *and a turtle. The top of the egg is marked with a crescent and stars; the bottom has small birds sitting on stalks of grass. The second 1869 egg shows a mug, a mallard, a potted bush, and insects when turned. The next egg has an axe in a tree, a plow and* 1870 *on the back, while the last egg reveals* SEG, April 8, 1880, *and a bird sitting on abstract flowers in a container.*

*Scratched by Susan Smyser, the left-hand egg rotates to reveal the date,* 1884, *and two additional flower sprays; the other egg of unknown origin exhibits a monument with a flag and the inscription,* Florrie 1860, 2½″ h.

sional or quite skilled; others are less studied or untutored-almost childlike (at left). Some designs are very boldly applied, while others are adept but light and spidery perhaps Victorian in feeling (p. 58).

Articles in women's periodicals offered suggestions for the decorating of the eggs with scratch carving beginning in 1872 with *Peterson's Ladies' Magazine* and continuing for approximately twenty years:

Besides those ornamented with decalcomania, you will wish to color a number with aniline dyes, which will give you every conceivable tint and shade of color; and these are exquisite with ferns, flowers, lettering, or simple sketches etched upon them.

To do this, draw a little vine for each side, and a picture for the centre, or, if you like, your name or monogram, or that of the person to whom you wish to give it, and then take a sharp-pointed pen-knife, and gently scrape away the color, lettering the figures in white upon the surface.

An Easter egg forms a still prettier gift if you scratch on it landscapes, or comic figures, or kindly mottoes, executed neatly with a sharp penknife. We have seen many of these scratched eggs made beautiful works of art. Choose a brown, crimson, or violet egg for this purpose, or at least one rather dark in colour, as the device appears in white. (*Cassell's,* Vol. III)

Eggs can also be beautifully colored with the dye which comes in ten-cent packages, and with a sharp penknife any design, flower, or name can be scratched on them. (*Our Homes,* 1888)

A neater and much better way than greasing the design, for those who do not mind the trouble, is to dye the egg all over, and then to scratch out the motto, or whatever is required white, with a penknife. This is, of course, a much more difficult process, and requires great care. (*Golden Days,* 1888)

A very pretty Easter gift is a boiled colored egg, on which, as on colored porcelain, the most various designs, monograms, pictures and the like, may be etched with a fine penknife. As hard-boiled eggs do not decompose, this forms a durable mark of remembrance. The brown color on our model, is produced by boiling the egg in water filled with onion peels. (*Good Housekeeping,* 1895)

With the directions for scratch-carving so widely distributed, it becomes more difficult to consider this type of decorated egg as a narrow cultural tradition.

ther suggestions for decorating the eggs included calico dyeing as recalled by Robert J. Burdette in *Ladies Home Journal* (1892):

A week before Easter somebody would go to the store to buy the calico with which to print the "aigs." "Is this fast colors?" and the clerk would lift his hand to heaven and swear that the deluge couldn't fade one of the brightest tints in the figure. After securing his affidavit we would tie the "aig" up in a bit of print and boil it. The calico would come out of the ordeal pure, spotless, whiter than snow, and the "aig" would be a thing of beauty in dots and leaves and twigs. "Oh, aig of the by-gone years!"

Another one required affixing plant material to the surface before dyeing as related in *Our Homes* (1888) and in *Golden Days* (March 24, 1888):

A pretty way is to grease a delicate piece of moss, a fine fern leaf, or a skeleton leaf; to roll either round a warm egg, so as to leave a greasy print on it, and then put it in the color; but great care must be taken in handling the work not to blur the design.

Eggs may be also simply treated by having small leaves or little bits of moss bound on to them with various colored wools or ribbons (not fast-colored ones), before they are boiled, the wool or ribbons being removed when they are dry again; the effect is often very good, but there is great doubt about the results in this way of coloring.

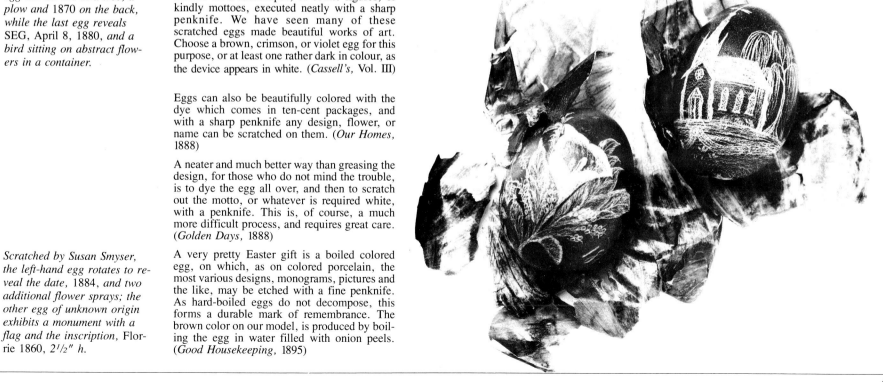

*Eggs for eating or giving were transformed with bits of lace, ribbon, silk, or crepe paper by following the suggestions offered in the April 1897 De-morest's. Courtesy: Library of Congress.*

"Etching" was one more way to embellish the egg according to *Youth's Companion* (March 21, 1878):

Often, then, we may wish a few white eggs, which are especially lovely among the bright colors. To have them exceedingly pretty, melt a little lard, and drop a piece of wax into it; to a cupful of lard, take a piece of wax as large as a walnut. Into this dip your egg, rolling it about so as to cover every part with the melted lard; then let it get cold.

Next take a sharp-pointed stick or a pen-knife, and very carefully cut out lines around the upper part of each end. Mark your monogram on one side, and a star or some other figure opposite to it.

Carefully scrape away all the lard and wax around the figure, and with a small camel's-hair brush dipped in turpentine, carefully clean the spots, wiping them with a soft rag on the end of a pointed stick. Have a cupful of the very strongest vinegar; put the egg in this and leave it until the shell is partly eaten away; then place it in hot water to melt off the grease.

The diamond dust that was sprinkled on Christmas ornaments was also employed for eggs as seen in *Youth's Companion* (March 21, 1878):

I will tell you of one more of this kind, with which we may make a charming nest. Take a few of your bright-colored eggs, and varnish them, and then, before they become quite dry, dust "diamond powder" or "frosting" all over the surface, or roll them in it.

For those talented, painting was a mode of decoration as these articles report in *Our Homes* (1888) and in *Golden Days* (1888):

Those who are skillful with pencil and paintbrush can present their friends with really exquisite souvenirs, by ornamenting eggs with flowers and butterflies, or appropriate texts of scripture. For these painted eggs, it is better to puncture a tiny hole with a pin in each side, and blow out the inside, leaving a clear shell, than to boil them; and the apertures can be concealed by stars of silver or gilt paper.

Eggs dyed pale blue, and little cloud and sea, with a tiny boat, painted on them, or dyed yellow and turned into a little sunset picture, with a tree added, are very pretty. They can be done in oil or water colors.

For more elaborate work, the eggs, having been boiled hard, can be painted over with gold size, and then covered with gold, or any metal leaf, which may be again painted on with oil paints, or, by using a medium and body colors, with water colors.

A gilt egg, with a white lily on it, or a silvered one with a daffodil, looks very pretty; violets and primroses, emblems of spring, are also appropriate, while eggs with butterflies or small birds bearing mottoes painted on them are much appreciated by children. When painted in water colors, the eggs can easily be varnished.

The use of rush-pith or binsa-graws for decorating eggs was not described in the periodicals studied, however Alfred Shoemaker reported its use in Pennsylvania. In addition, Venetia Newall noted that decorating the egg with the rush-pith was common to western Poland and Silesia where intricate patterns of the plant material were applied, sometimes in combination with wool. She also stated that Moravians appliqued the eggs and used them as toys, putting pebbles inside and hanging them over cribs. In Pennsylvania the binsa graws eggs were deco-

rated in two styles, both simpler than their European counterparts. The style practiced by Viola Miller was to wrap the entire egg with pith and then to apply figures cut from patterned material to the wrapped egg, forming a design such as eggs in a basket or birds on a branch. The other tradition continued by Laura Huyett was to first cover the egg with cloth and then to outline patterns on the cloth with the pith, creating geometic or free-form designs. Fanny Bankus decorated eggs in this manner as a child in Lancaster and continued to do so after she married Joseph Catherman and lived in Laurelton. Two of her granddaughters, Gladys (Mrs. John L.) Coleman and Olive (Mrs. John F.) Stamm, have three of the eggs Fanny made in 1920. According to some, the bulrush which grows in marshy fields must be cut in the full moon, or it will be empty. Once the grass-like spikes are cut, the outside is split. A wooden matchstick or other small diameter rod can be inserted into the inch-long split. With a gentle motion, the stick is pushed the length of the reed, causing the cream-colored pith to pop out, splitting the reed as it comes. The lengths are then used while still pliable to cover the egg. Viola Miller learned the tradition from an elderly Myerstown woman who had practiced the art as a child. Both women claimed that homecooked flour and water paste was the only glue that performed well (p. 61).

Just as the publications of the 1870s and the 1880s concentrated on the dyeing and decorating of the eggs, the next three decades emphasized the application of paper to the egg to create historic and national figures like Josephine, Napoleon and Chinamen. Pretty ladies in bonnets and animals were also popular subjects for the eggs; directions for roosters, bunnies, frogs and turtles were most commonly given (left). In contrast to the familiar, designers seem to vie with each other to create patterns for the most hideous and grotesque creatures that could be imagined.

Eventually, eggs of glass, wood, chocolate, marshmallow, lithographed tin, spun sugar, and plastic replaced the traditional dyed chicken egg. It is now enjoying a revival of interest created by contemporary egg scratchers. The photograph at the right contains a sampler of women's work today (from left to right in a clockwise manner): Joan Maurer, New Berlin/bird and flower; Evelyn Althouse, Ephrata/vines; Barbara Brubaker Bomberger, Manheim/reverse technique, bird; Ingrid Steffensen, Lewisburg/unicorn; Barbara Bomberger/geometric, beehive; Ann Zawacki, Bradford/flower; Marie Foust, Watsontown/bunnies and flowers; Nada Gray, Lewisburg/*Joan;* Evelyn Althouse/bird on flower; Jeannette Lasansky, Lewisburg/stylized flowers; Eleanor Leitch, Baltimore/bird and flowers; and Marie Foust/feathers. Of the craftpeople represented, Evelyn Althouse was one of the first to revive the art, teaching and demonstrating at the Pennsylvania Farm Museum. Barbara Bomberger was active as recently as fifteen years ago. Ann Zawacki is one contemporary artist that markets eggs at craft fairs similar to the Lewisburg Festival of the Arts. Marie Foust, one of the most recent but most devoted practitioners of the Pennsylvania-German art, demonstrates and teaches throughout Pennsylvania from Bedford at Bedford Village to the Mercer Museum Craft Fair in Doylestown. She has completed more than three hundred eggs picturing flowers, birds, crosses, scenes, and animals. One of the Watsontown artist's proudest moments was her acceptance by the jury of the Pennsylvania Guild of Craftsmen in 1982–their first egg scratcher.

Marie Foust, as well as the other women represented, uses natural dyes for the eggs, predominately onion skins and red cabbage. To prepare a dye bath, the plant material must be collected and cut or shredded, placed in a stainless steel, granite, or heat proof glass container (never aluminum), and covered with water. Most egg scratchers prefer to put the eggs in the pan with the dye materials and to simmer both for thirty minutes which produces interesting patterns of color. In contrast, Evelyn Althouse prefers to simmer the material for one hour or longer until the color looks deep enough, then to strain the dye bath, and let it cool. The dye bath can be used cold or can be simmered with eggs until they reach the desired tint. Eggs should then be rinsed and allowed to drain dry.

Dyeing the eggs can be exciting and frustrating. Working with natural or vegetable dyes is not a science, no result is guaranteed, and no color is repeated even if measurements are strictly followed. Egg shells vary in their ability to absorb dyes; plant materials differ in their concentrations of color. Red cabbage, which can yield a pleasing deep blue, can also produce a pale tint. It is the most unreliable of the plant materials and also fades the most rapidly. Karen Roszel of Danville recommends boiling the eggs in cabbage water and leaving them in that solution overnight. Goldenrod produces a warm yellow; the entire dandelion plant, a pale yellow; walnut hulls, a rich brown. All dye materials work best in the presence of a mordant or metal salt. Household mordants–alum, cream of tartar, or vinegar should be thoroughly mixed with the dye solution before the eggs are added. Use one tablespoon of the mordant in one quart of dye. For further information on vegetable dyes consult books on wool and cotton dyeing.

Eggs for dyeing must be clean. Wash with a mixture of one cup of warm water and one tablespoon of white vinegar, scrubbing lightly with a terry cloth rag. Rinse the eggs well in clear water and dry carefully. The eggs and the dye bath must be the same temperature or the eggs will crack.

Traditionally the egg was used whole. If left undisturbed, the white of the egg would dry leaving a hard yolk which would rattle when gently shaken. The egg could also weep, causing an unpleasant odor, or it could explode emitting strong sulphuric fumes. According to Edwin M. Fogel it was believed that presentation eggs kept longer than a year would bring the recipient bad luck. Not so much concerned with superstition, most professionals who sell their eggs are not willing to risk the explosion which can result so they blow their eggs before dyeing or use raw eggs, a cold dye bath, and blow them afterwards. Blown eggs are difficult to keep submerged in the dye bath unless filled with the cold dye before simmering or weighted in some other manner. Also since blowing the egg can result in a larger than desired opening, some suggest using a small craft drill, others rely on the accepted pin, while still others use a large hypodermic needle and syringe, which can also act as a suction to drain the egg.

Except for a few women like Marilyn Opelt Mosheim and Mary Kocher Bogar, both third generation scratchers, Pennsylvania-German women have had to learn by trial and error for the craft was a lost art. However, today with a renewed interest in our heritage, demonstrators can be found at ethnic folk festivals and traditional eggs can again be included in the nest.

*Teachers and their students perpetuate the art of scratch-carving eggs as illustrated by these contemporary eggs, 2"- 3¹/₂" h.*

## Published Sources/General

Adams, William T. *Our Little Ones: Illustrated Stories and Poems of Little People.* Boston: Lee and Shepard, 1880-1883.

*American Agriculturist.* December 1861, 1865, 1869, and October, 1865.

*American Heritage Cookbook and Illustrated History of American Eating and Drinking.* New York: Simon and Schuster, 1964.

*Anti-Masonic Star.* New Berlin, Pennsylvania, April 17, 1835-December 4, 1835.

*Arthur's Ladies' Magazine.* Philadelphia: E. Ferret and Company, 1857-1859.

Beard, Lina and Adelia B. *What a Girl Can Make and Do.* New York: Charles Scribner's and Sons, 1920.

_____. *Things Worth Doing and How To Do Them.* New York: Charles Scribner's and Sons, 1906.

Beecher, Catherine Esther. *Treatise on Domestic Economy.* New York: Harper and Brothers, 1847 revised.

_____. *The New Housekeeper's Manual.* New York: J. B. Ford and Company, 1873.

Beecher, Mrs. W. H. *All Around the House or How to Make a Home Happy.* New York: C. Appleton and Company, 1879.

*The Book of the Household or Family Dictionary.* London and New York: The London Printing and Publishing Company, Limited, n.d.

*Cassell's Book of the Household, A Work of Reference on Domestic Economy.* II. London, Paris, and Melbourne: Cassell and Company, Ltd., n.d.

*Cassell's Household Guide.* I-IV. London and New York: Cassell, Pelter and Galpin, n.d.

Clarke, J. Erskine, ed. *Chatterbox.* Boston: Estes and Lauriat, 1893-1906.

Cox, Edward Young. *Garnishing Churches at Christmas and Other Festivals.* London: Cox and Company, 1920.

Crane, Walter. *A Wonder Book for Girls and Boys.* Boston: Houghton Mifflin and Company, 1851.

*The Delineator.* New York: Ebenezer Butterick, 1875, 1885, 1891-1893, 1896-1899.

*Demorest's Family Magazine.* New York: J. J. Little and Company, 1865-1899 except 1883, 1887.

Gardner, Pat and Kay Gleason. *Dough Creations, Food to Folk Art.* Radnor, Pennsylvania: Chilton Book Company, 1977.

Gay, Kathlyn. *The Germans Helped Build America.* United States and Canada: Julian Messner, 1971.

*Godey's Lady's Book.* Philadelphia, 1831-1834, 1841-1843, 1845, 1849-1853, 1855-1859,

1860-1863, 1865-1872, 1875, 1880, 1888-1889, and 1892-1893.

*Golden Days for Boys and Girls.* Philadelphia: James Elverson, 1880-1892.

Goodholme, Todd S., ed. *A Domestic Cyclopedia of Practical Information.* New York: Henry Holt and Company, 1877.

*Good Housekeeping.* New York, 1885-1908.

*The Goshenhoppen Newsletter.* Green Lane, Pennsylvania: Goschenhoppen Historians, Inc., December, 1981.

*Graham's Magazine.* Philadelphia, December, 1844, 1848, and 1851-1853.

Grief, Martin. *The Holiday Book.* New York: The Main Street Press, Universe Books, 1978.

Harbaugh, Henry. *The Guardian.* Lewisburg-Lancaster, Pennsylvania, I-XVIII, 1850-1867.

*Harper's Bazar.* New York, 1879-1895.

*Harper's New Monthly Magazine.* New York, 1856-1892.

*Harper's Weekly.* New York, 1857-1888.

*Harper's Young People.* New York, 1876-1895.

Harrowven, Jean. *Origins of Festivals and Feasts.* London: Kaye and Ward Ltd., 1980.

Hartley, Florence. *The Ladies' Handbook of Fancy and Ornamental Work.* Philadelphia: G. G. Evans, 1860.

Hassard, Annie. *Floral Decoration for the Dwelling House.* London and New York: Macmillan and Company, 1876.

*Horticulturist.* 1849-1850.

Hostetler, John A., *Amish Society.* Baltimore: Johns Hopkins Press, 1981.

Houts, Thomas. "The Volunteer Bands of Hummelstown, 1869-1927." *Pennsylvania Heritage,* Harrisburg, Pennsylvania: Pennsylvania Historical and Museum Commission, VIII:3, Summer, 1982.

Howard, Marian B. *Those Fascinating Paper Dolls, An Illustrated Handbook for Collectors.* New York: Dover Publications, Inc., 1981.

Hulbert, Anne, *Victorian Crafts Revived.* New York: Hastings House, Publishers, 1978.

*Intelligencer.* Danville, Pennsylvania, July 5, 1828-November 22, 1861, and September 20, 1872-July 4, 1879.

Jones, Mrs. C. S. and Henry T. Williams. *Household Elegancies.* New York: Henry T. Williams, 1875.

_____. *Ladies Fancy Work.* III. New York: Henry T. Williams, 1876.

Jones, R. G. "A Standard Dictionary of English Folk Tales," *Journal of the Society for Folk Life Studies.* Tudor Works, Cardiff: Qualitch Printing Limited, 1972.

Judd, David W. *Our Homes—How to Beautify Them.* New York: D. Judd Co., 1888.

Kirsch, Francine. *Chromos, A Guide to Paper Collectibles.* La Jolla, California: A. S. Barnes and Company, Inc., 1981.

Kulp, Isaac Clarence. *The Goschenhoppen Region.* Green Lane, Pennsylvania: The Goschenhoppen Historians, Inc., I:2, 1978.

*Ladies Home Journal.* Philadelphia: Curtis Publishing Co., 1883-1924.

*Lady's Friend.* Philadelphia, December, 1868.

Lambert, Miss. *The Hand-book of Needlework.* New York: Wiley and Putnam, 1842.

Lasansky, Jeannette. *To Cut, Piece, and Solder.* Lewisburg, Pennsylvania: Oral Traditions Project, 1982.

Leslie, Miss Eliza. *The House Book.* Philadelphia: Carey and Hart, 1840.

*Frank Leslie's Illustrated Newspaper.* New York: December, 1863, 1867-1868, 1875-1879, 1883, and 1885.

*Lewisburg Chronicle.* Lewisburg, Pennsylvania, June 6, 1865-December 30, 1886.

*Lewisburg Chronicle and Union County General Advertiser.* Lewisburg, Pennsylvania, July 17, 1847-December 11, 1847.

*Lewisburg Chronicle and Union County Star.* Lewisburg, Pennsylvania, May 6, 1859-December 30, 1864.

*Lewisburg Chronicle and West Branch Farmer.* Lewisburg, Pennsylvania, December 25, 1847-April 29, 1859.

*Lewisburg Democrat.* Lewisburg, Pennsylvania, January 20, 1835-February 27, 1836; December 1, 1852-January 5, 1853; and June 1, 1853-December 27, 1854.

*Lewisburg Journal.* Lewisburg, Pennsylvania, January 8, 1830-October 30, 1832.

*Lewisburg Journal and Union County Advocate.* Lewisburg, Pennsylvania, February 18, 1833-February 22, 1834.

*Lewisburg Saturday News.* Lewisburg, Pennsylvania, June 4, 1887-October 13, 1888.

*Lewisburg Standard.* Lewisburg, Pennsylvania, December 7, 1837-December 11, 1839.

McCulloch, Lou W. *Paper Americana, A Collector's Guide,* New York: A. S. Barnes and Company, Inc., 1980.

Meyers, Robert J. *Celebrations: The Complete Book of American Holidays.* Garden City, New York: Doubleday and Company, Inc., 1972.

*Middleburg Post.* Middleburg, Pennsylvania: 1870-1873; 1877; 1879-1880 except March, April, May, and June; 1880-1882; 1883; 1892 except September and October; 1896 except October; 1906 except December 13; and 1910 except April, October, and November.

*Mifflinburg Telegraph.* Mifflinburg, Pennsylvania: June 10, 1862-October 29, 1884.

*Dr. Miles' Candy Book.* n.p., n.d.

*Modern Priscilla.* 1887-1880, 1890-1895.

*Montour American.* Danville, Pennsylvania, February 2, 1871-May 24, 1878.

*Muncy Luminary and Lycoming County Advertiser.* Muncy, Pennsylvania, April 10, 1841-January 2, 1880, except December 31, 1842-July 7, 1843; July 22, 1843-March 2, 1844; and September 7, 1844.

Ossoli, Margaret Fuller. *Woman in the Nineteenth Century and Kindred Papers.* Boston: John D. Jewett and Co., 1855.

*Our Young People.* Milwaukee, Wisconsin, December 28, 1894.

Owen, Trefor M. *Welsh Folk Customs.* National Museum of Wales, 1978.

*Paper and Scissors in the Schoolroom.* Boston: Milton Bradley, 1893.

*Pennsylvania Folklore Society.* VI, 1941.

*The Pennsylvania-German.* December, 1906.

*Peoples' Advocate.* August 7, 1838-April 9, 1841.

*Peterson's Ladies' National Magazine.* Philadelphia, 1842-1893.

Pieske, Christa. "The Fabrication of Luxury Paper in Berlin Since 1900." *Volkskunst,* August, 1978.

*Polish Customs.* Detroit, Michigan: Friends of Polish Art, 1979.

Porter, Glen and William H. Mulligan, Jr. ed. "Industrious Women. Home and Work in the Nineteenth-Century—Mid-Atlantic Region." *Working Papers from the Regional Economic History Research Center.* Greenville, Delaware: Eleutherian Mills-Hagley Foundation, V:2, 3 1982.

*Practical Information.* New York: Henry Holt and Company, 1877.

Reed, C. A., Company. *Catalogs.* Williamsport, Pennsylvania: C. A. Reed Co., 1949, 1950, 1952, 1953, 1959.

Rogers, Barbara Radcliffe. *An Introduction of Twenty-One Traditional Yankee Home Crafts.* Dublin, New Hampshire: Yankee, Inc., 1979.

Rombauer, Irma S. *The Joy of Cooking.* Philadelphia: The Blakiston Company, 1943.

Ryan, Dorothy B. *Picture Postcards in the United States 1892-1918.* New York: Clarkson N. Potter, Inc., 1982.

*Saint Nicholas, Scribner's Illustrated Magazine for Girls and Boys.* New York: Scribner and Company, I, II, IV, VI, and VII, November 1873-October 1880.

*Schoolday Visitor.* Philadelphia: J. W. Daughaday, February and October, 1869; January, 1870; January, February, March and August, 1871.

*Scrap Reliefs.* Suffolk, England: Mamelok Press Ltd., n.d.

*Selingsgrove Times.* Selinsgrove, Pennsylvania, August 22, 1873–November 5, 1891.

Simmons, Amelia, "An American Orphan" *American Cookery.* West Virginia Pulp and Paper Company, 1963.

Sirkis, Susan. *The Wishbooklet.* XII. West Point, New York: n.p., 1973.

Stewart, Ellinore, Pruitt. *Letters of a Woman Homesteader.* Boston: Houghton Mifflin, 1982.

Stowe, Catherine E. Beecher and Harriet Beecher Stowe. *The American Woman's Home.* Watkins Glen, New York: Library of Victorian Culture, American Life Foundation, 1970.

Stowe, Harriet Beecher. *The Writings of Harriet Beecher Stowe in Sixteen Volumes.* Cambridge, Massachusetts: Houghton Mifflin and Company, 1896.

Tibbott, S. Menevel. *Welsh Fare: A Selection of Traditional Recipes.* Cowbridge and Bridgend, Glamorgan: D. Brown and Sons Limited, 1976.

*Trials and Confession of An American Housekeeper.* Philadelphia: Lippincott, Geanko and Company, 1854.

Trowbridge, J. T., ed. *Our Young Folks, An Illustrated Magazine for Boys and Girls, Volume II.* Boston: Ticknor and Fields, 1866.

Tudor, Tasha. *A Time to Keep.* Chicago, New York, and San Francisco: Rand McNally and Company, 1977.

Tudor, Tasha and Linda Allen. *Old-Fashioned Gifts.* New York: David McKay Company, Inc., 1979.

*Union Argus.* Lewisburg, Pennsylvania, July 31, 1855–October 11, 1860.

*Union Hickory.* Lewisburg, Pennsylvania, February 17, 1829–April 3, 1830.

*Union Star.* New Berlin, Pennsylvania, March 7, 1840–March 7, 1850.

*Union Telegraph.* New Berlin, Pennsylvania, April 24, 1827–July 13, 1832.

*Union Times.* New Berlin, Pennsylvania, August 28, 1824–December 3, 1845.

*Union Weekly.* Lewisburg, Pennsylvania, September 19, 1833–July 22, 1834.

Vick, James Seedman. *Vick's Illustrated.* Rochester, New York, February, 1878–July, 1891.

*Weekly Herald.* Adamsburg, Pennsylvania, March 5, 1887–July 22, 1888; July 14, 1892–December 31, 1916.

Weygandt, Cornelius. *The Dutch Country.* New York, London: D. Appleton-Century, Co., 1939.

*Woman's Home Companion.* Cleveland: Crowell Publishing Company, 1897–1927.

*The Youth's Companion.* Boston: Perry Mason and Company, 1870, 1871, 1873–1875, 1878–1880, 1902, 1903, and 1906.

Zeitlin, Steven J., Amy J. Kotkin, and Holly Cutting Baker. *A Celebration of American Family Folklore.* New York: Pantheon Books, 1982.

## Published Sources/Christmas

*The Atlantic Souvenir: Christmas and New Year's Offering.* Philadelphia: Carey, Lea and Carey, 1828.

Auld, William Muir. *Christmas Traditions.* New York: The Macmillan Company, 1931.

Bangs, John Kendrick. *A Little Book of Christmas.* Boston: Little Brown and Company, 1912.

Barnett, James H. *The American Christmas.* New York: Macmillan, 1954.

Caldwell, Dorothy J. "Christmases in Early Missouri." *Missouri Historical Review,* LXV:2, January, 1971.

Campbell, R. J. *The Story of Christmas.* New York: The Macmillan Company, 1935.

"Children's Books to Comics." *Encyclopedia of Collectibles.* Alexandria, Virginia: Time-Life Books, 1978.

"Christmas at Greenfield Village and Henry Ford Museum." *American Antiques,* V:12, December 1977.

*Christmas Blossoms and New Years Wreath of Uncle Thomas.* Philadelphia: E. H. Butler and Company, 1849.

*A Christmas Box.* New York: R. Worthington, 1880.

*Christmas for Tots.* New York: Elton and Company, 1840.

*The Christmas Locket.* Boston: Roberts Brothers, 1870.

"Christmas in Lancaster in 1874." *Journal of the Lancaster County Historical Society,* LXXI:4, 1967.

Mrs. Clarke. *Christmas Eve at Dusslethal.* London: B. Wertheim Aldine Chambers, 1847.

Court, Earl W. *4000 Years of Christmas.* New York: Schuman, 1948.

Crippen, T. G. *Christmas and Christmas Lore.* London: Blackic, 1923.

Dawson, William Francis. *Christmas: Its Origin and Associations.* London: Elliot Stock, 1902.

Elsbeth. "Victorian Ornaments." Cumberland, Maryland: Hobby House Press, 1975.

Faust, Joan Lee. "Centuries of Historic Tradition Trim the Christmas Tree." *New York Times, December, 1979.*

Foley, Daniel J. *Christmas in the Good Old Days.* Philadelphia and New York: Chilton Company, 1961.

_____. *Christmas the World Over.* Philadelphia: Chilton, 1963.

_____. *The Christmas Tree.* Philadelphia: Chilton, 1960.

Green, *Nursery Keepsake.* n.p., 1850.

Greene, J. B. *An Adventure of Santa Claus.* Boston: Lee and Shepard, 1871.

Greenwood, Grace. *The Little Pilgrim.* Philadelphia: n.p., 1896.

Haugan, Randolph E. *Christmas.* Minneapolis: Augsburg Publishing House, 1-L, 1931–1980.

Hornung, Clarence P. *An Old-Fashioned Christmas in Illustration and Decoration.* New York: Dover Publications, 1975.

*The House.* London, December. 1901.

Hubbard, Clarence T. "Christmases of Victorian Days." *Antiques Journal,* XXIII:12, December, 1968.

Jones, E. Willis. *The Santa Claus Book.* New York: Walker and Company, 1976.

Jordan, Mildred. *Apple in the Attic.* New York: Grosset and Dunlap, 1942.

Kainen, Ruth Cole. *America's Christmas Heritage.* New York: Funk and Wagnalls, 1969.

Keiffer, Elizabeth Clarke. "Christmas Customs of Lancaster County." *Journal of the Lancaster County Historical Society,* XLIV, 1940.

Krythe, Maymie R. *All About Christmas.* New York: Harper, 1954.

*Lancaster Echoes.* Lancaster, Pennsylvania, I:6, December–January, 1980-81.

"Lauscha." *Gaffer.* Corning, New York: Corning Glass Works, December, 1946.

*Frank Leslie's Christmas Book.* New York: Mrs. Frank Leslie, 1881–1887.

McKinley, Sue and Barbara French. *Christmas Creations at Eleutherian Mills.* Greeneville, Delaware: Eleutherian Mills-Hagley Mills-Hagley Foundation, 1977.

Mercer, Mrs. William R. "Origin and Customs of Christmas Festivals." *Collections of Papers Read Before the Bucks County Historical Society,* III, 1909.

Meyer, Priscilla S. *Christmas Inside Old Houses.* Armonk, New York: Oak Cottage Farm, 1981.

Miall, Anthony and Peter. *The Victorian Christmas Book.* New York: Pantheon Books, 1978.

Miles, Clement A. *Christmas in Ritual and Tradition, Christian and Pagan.* London: Unwin, 1912.

O'Neil, Sunny. *The Gift of Christmas Past: A Return to Victorian Traditions.* Nashville, Tennessee: American Association for State and Local History, 1981.

*The Pennsylvania Dutchman.* Lancaster, Pennsylvania: Pennsylvania Dutch Folklore Center, Inc., December, 1949; December 15, 1950.

Robacker, Earl R. "Back Along." *Pennsylvania Folklife.* Lancaster, Pennsylvania: Pennsylvania Folklife Society, Inc., XVI:2, Winter, 1966–1967.

Rogers, Maggie and Judith Hawkins. *The Glass Christmas Ornament: Old and New.* Forest Grove, Oregon: Timber Press, 1977.

Ronsheim, Robert. "Christmas at Conner Prairie." *History News.* XXXVI:12, December, 1981.

Rubenstein, Lewis C. "Victorian Christmas Greens." *Antiques.* December, 1959.

Ruland, Joseph. *Christmas in Germany.* Bonn: Howacht, 1978.

*Saint Nicholas Book.* Clinton, New Jersey: Main Street Press, Universe Books, 1976.

Scharer, Laura Lynne. "Christmas Past—How to Decorate Historical Trees." *History News.* Nashville, Tennessee: American Association of State and Local History, December, 1980.

Schreiber, William T. "First American Christmas Tree," *The American-German Review,* X:2, December 2, 1943.

Shoemaker, Alfred L. *Christmas in Pennsylvania: A Folk-Culture Study.* Kutztown, Pennsylvania: Pennsylvania Folklife Society, 1959.

Shuart, Harry Wilson. "From Beads to Baubles." *Spinning Wheel,* XXVI:10, December, 1970.

Snyder, Phillip V. *The Christmas Tree Book.* New York: The Viking Press, 1976.

Sterbenz, Carol Endler and Nancy Johnson. *The Decorated Tree.* New York: Harry N. Abrams, Inc., 1982.

Thackery, William Makepeace. *Roundabout Papers.* New York: Harper and Brothers, 1863.

*Treasured Polish Customs.* Minneapolis, Minnesota: n.p., 1980.

Weiser, Francis X. *Handbook of Christian Feasts and Customs.* New York: Harcourt, Brace, 1952.

Wernecke, Herbert H. *Christmas Customs Around the World.* Philadelphia: Westminster Press, 1959.

Yoder, Don. "Christmas Customs: Folk Cultural Questionnaire No. 10." *Pennsylvania Folklife.* Lancaster, Pennsylvania: Pennsylvania Folklife Society, Inc., XVIII:2, Winter, 1968-69.

*Yuletide at Winterthur, Tastes and Visions of the Season.* Winterthur, Delaware: The Henry Francis du Pont Winterthur Museum, 1980.

## Published Sources/Easter

Best, Martha. "Easter Customs in Lehigh Valley." *Pennsylvania Folklife.* Lancaster, Pennsylvania: Pennsylvania Folklife Society, Inc., XLII:3, Spring 1968.

Coskey, Evelyn. *Easter Eggs for Everyone.* New York, Nashville: Abingdon Press, 1973.

Crolsman, Neil R. "Wycinanki and Pysanky: forms of religious and ethnic folk art from the Delaware Valley." Pittsburgh: Pennsylvania Ethnic Heritage Center, 1981.

Doane, W. C. *The Book of Easter.* New York: The Macmillan Company, 1910.

*Egg Art.* Washington, D. C.: American Folklife Center, The Library of Congress, 1982.

Gacek, Anna Zajac. *Pisanki.* New Bedford, Massachusetts: Sarmatia Publications, 1979.

Györgyi, Erzsébet Jöldes. "Metallapplizerte Eier Aus Umgarn." *Volkskunst,* 1982.

Hazeltine, Alice Isabel and Elva Sophronia Smith. *The Easter Book of Legends and Stories.* New York: Lothrop, Lee and Shepard Co., 1947.

Johnson, David. *Natural Dye Notebook.* Commonwealth of Pennsylvania, 1976.

Johnson, Kathryn E. "Egg Decorating at the Kutztown Folk Festival." *Pennsylvania Folklife.* Collegeville, Pennsylvania: Pennsylvania Folklife Society, Inc., XXXI:4, Summer 1982.

Kieffer, Elizabeth Clarke. "Easter Customs of Lancaster County." *Papers of the Lancaster County Historical Society,* LII:3, 1948.

Kirkland, Winifred. *The Easter People.* New York: Fleming H. Revell Company, 1923.

König, Wolfhilde. "Oesterliche Gebrauchsgraphik." *Volkskunst,* May, 1978.

Lord, Priscilla and Daniel J. Foley. *Easter Garland.* Philadelphia: Chilton, 1963.

——. *Easter the World Over.* Philadelphia: Chilton, 1971.

Luciw, Wasyl O. and George Wynnysky. "The Ukranian Pysanka and Other Decorative Easter Eggs in Pennsylvania." *Pennsylvania Folklife.* Lancaster, Pennsylvania: Pennsylvania Folklife Society, Inc., XXI:3, Spring, 1972.

Mitz, Anne, ed. *Ukranian Arts.* New York: Ukranian Youth's League of North America, Inc., 1955.

Newall, Venetia. *An Egg at Easter.* Bloomington, Indiana: Indiana University Press, 1971.

Newsome, Arden. *Egg Decorating, Plain and Fancy.* New York: Crown Publishers, Inc., 1973.

newspaper files. Chester County Historical Society.

Overdorf, Karen. "Woman Modifies Ukranian Method to Decorate Eggs." *Daily Item,* Sunbury, Pennsylvania, March 28, 1975.

——. "She Practices Ancient Ukranian Egg Art." *Daily Item,* Sunbury, Pennsylvania, March 28, 1975.

Patton, Judith. "Giving Decorated Chicken Eggs at Easter Festival is Centuries Old." *Sunday Patriot News,* Harrisburg, Pennsylvania, March 29, 1970.

*The Pennsylvania Dutchman.* Lancaster, Pennsylvania: The Pennsylvania Dutch Folklore Center, Inc., IV:15, Easter, 1953.

Rice, Susan Tracy, *Easter.* New York: Dodd Mead and Company, 1916.

"Scratch-Carved Eggs." *Colonial Homes.* New York: The Hearst Corporation, XVIII:2, March-April, 1982.

"Scratch-Carved Eggs." *Creative Crafts.* n.p., April, 1975.

Sechrist, Elizabeth Hough and Jane Hewoolsey. *It's Time for Easter.* Philadelphia: Macnie Smith Company, 1961.

Shoemaker, Alfred L. *Eastertide in Pennsylvania.* Kutztown, Pennsylvania: Pennsylvania Folklife Society, 1960.

Sonntag, Linda, *Eggs.* New York: G. P. Putnam's and Sons, 1980.

Ward, Don. "Class in Pysanky Unscrambles the Art of Ukranian Egg Decorating." *The Catholic Witness.* March 11, 1976.

Weygandt, Cornelius. *The Blue Hills.* New York: Henry Holt and Company, Inc., 1936.

## Unpublished Sources

Diaries/Chester County Historical Society, West Chester, Pennsylvania: Peirce, Hannah Greaves, E. Marlboro, 1771–1781; Walton, Mary, 1816–1817; Bowman, Deborah, 1832; Brinton, Cassandra, 1840–1866; Charton, May Ann, 1844–1849; Mercer, Margaretta J., Kennett Square, 1850; Brinton, Gulielma, 1850–1879; Gotchall, Sarah, 1851; Doane, Elizabeth, 1852–1853; Wickersham, Phebe G., Marlboro, Chester, 1855; Yeatman, Lavinia Passmore, Kennett, 1855–1856; Hopkins, Mary Brinton, 1855–1857; Wilson, Susan E., 1855–1861; Walton, Lizzie T., 1856–1858; King, Agnes Thomas, 1856–1885; Carpenter, Annie R., Northbrook—Marshalltown area, 1857–1864; Lamborn, Anna M., 1860–1865; Davis, Janetta, 1860–1878; Zook, Mary T., West Whitelava Twp., 1861, 1872; Wood, Philie C., 1862; Williamson, Clara, 1863–1867; Greenfield, E. Jane, London Grove Twp; Roberts, Sarah Jane, London Grove, 1863–1903; Wood, Philena C., Steelville, 1864; Zook, Mary T., 1865–1869; Lamborn, Hannah Mary, 1865–1870; Garrett, Anna M., 1865–1890; Palmer, Mary S., West Chester, 1864–1866; Sheeder, Anna M., E. Vincent Twp., 1870–1879; Sheeder, Nancy Jane, 1871; Wood, Lydia, 1871, 1872; Tutton, Elizabeth J.,

Downington, 1872, 1877, 1896; Harvey, Cassandra, 1874–1882; Marshall, Mary, 1878–1883; Hawley, Catharine, West Chester, 1883; Tanguy, Kate, West Chester, 1881–1913; Mercer, Lydia, Williston, 1884–1886; Baldwin, Jennie, 1886–1887; Linville, Emma Henderson, Lancaster, 1886–1887; Clark, Mary, 1895.

Pennsylvania Historical and Museum Commission, Archives, Harrisburg, Pennsylvania: Brisbane, John, 1770–1824; Potts, Stacy, Jr., 1798–1799; Groninger, Jacob, 1831–1891; Anonymous, Memo book, 1832–1833; Hans, Pliny, 1851–1853; Anonymous farmer, 1851–1853; Werst, Elizabeth, Mechanicsburg, 1854, 1858, 1865–1880; Kerr, Jonathan Williams, 1862–1865; Koeper, John F., 1862–1864, 1871; Egle, William Henry, 1863–1865; Hurst, Templeton Bardon, 1864–1865; Squires, A. N., Pompey-McKean County, 1864–1896; Anonymous Painter, Leesport, 1867; Lehmer, Jacob F., 1871–1914; Wissler, Aaron, Lancaster, 1872, 1875, 1878, 1881–1894, 1899–1902; Hein, Aaron D., Elizabethtown, 1881; Knepp, George L. Hollidaysburg, 1890–1907.

Letters/Private Collection: Lincoln, Richard Van Buskirk, Family Letters, 1870–1880.

Manuscripts/Union County Historical Society, Lewisburg, Pennsylvania: Bikle, Emma Wolf, Christmas Lists, 1885–1897; Schopfer, Marilyn. "History of C. A. Reed Company," Williamsport, Pennsylvania; Simkins, Emma C. "Christmas Customs in the Colonies," DAR paper prepared for the Zebulon Pike Chaper, Colorado, n.d.

Pennsylvania Folklife Collection, Ursinus College, Ursinus Pennsylvania: Shoemaker, Alfred L. Folk Cultural Collection.

Group Interviews/Union-Snyder County Senior Citizen Centers at Beaver Springs on February 24 and April 22, 1981; Lewisburg on December 10, 1980 and April 5, 1981; Middleburg on February 20 and April 9, 1981; Mifflinburg on December 9, 1980 and March 11, 1981; New Columbia on December 2, 1980 and March 7, 1981; Selinsgrove on February 23, April 20 and June 16, 1981; and Riverview Manor at the United Methodist Home, Lewisburg, on November 13, 1980.

Individual Interviews/Harry Ammon, Judy Hixson Anderson, Connie Wirt Bastian, Jennie Bingaman, Grace Huntington Bennett, Mary Kocher Bogar, Hazel Bergenstock Burrey, John Catherman, Evelyn and Matt Chabal, Margaret Gutelius

Chambers, William and Martha Conrad, Harold M. Danowsky, Mary DeFrain Danowsky, Alma Dewire, Lulu Miller Dieffenderfer, David Dunn, Ruth Criswell Eisenhauer, Maude Engle, Carol Ewing, Clair Groover, Marguerite Hackenburg, Pauline Hoffman Hause, Willis Hause, Helen Hoffa, Marcia Hoffman, Grant Hoopert, Olive Thompson Hoover, Robert Hoover, Norma Howland, Marguerite Libby Keister, Marguerite Alstadt Kieffer, Murray Kline, Grace Hassinger Klose, Rhoda and William Ladd, Merrill Linn, Grace Zimmerman Lohr, Mary Ruhl Maher, Lillian Worrell Minnich, Annie Morgalis, Marilyn Opelt Mosheim, Malcolm Musser, Thomas Musser, Julia Nichols, Lib Spyker Owens, Corrine and William Pauza, Bee Eaker Petrie, Janet Soars Platt, Paulene Huntington Poggi, Martha Herman Pontius, Kenneth Reish, Donald Rote, Ernest Ruhl, Ethel Dieffenderfer Ruhl, Mary Naugle Sassaman, Amelia Schell Schnure, Marion Albright Sechler, Florence Catherman Shively, Kathryn Glover Shoemaker, Verna Erdley Sholter, Helen Moyer Shriner, Winifred Smith, Ada Delcamp Snyder, Blanche Burns Snyder, Catherine Snyder, Charles McCool Snyder, Martha Courter Snyder, Mary Burrowes Snyder, Cheryl Mader Sowul, Dale Spangler, Elmer Stahl, Eric Stewart, Harry Stuck, Myrtle Thompson, Ferne Shirk Troxell, Arlena Moyer Wagner, Blanche Marks Walter, Laura Emery Walter, Naomi Tharp Weidensaul, Marie Shiffer Wolfe, Cecile Boyer Young, Lib Smith Zimmerman.

Correspondence/Evelyn Althouse, Ephrata, Pennsylvania; Mrs. Russell B. Baver, Topton, Pennsylvania; Carolyn A. Bercier, Gallier House, New Orleans, Louisiana; Roberta Bradford, Stowe-Day Foundation, Hartford, Connecticut; Catherine M. Brosky, Carnegie Library, Pittsburgh, Pennsylvania; Andreas Brown, Gotham Book Mart and Gallery, Inc., New York; Clyde L. Bunce, Williamsport, Pennsylvania; Elaine Chessman, Mark Twain Memorial, Hartford, Connecticut; Wendie Christie, Philadelphia Museum of Art, Philadelphia, Pennsylvania; Malcolm Clinger, Lewisburg, Pennsylvania; Carolyn H. Cockrell, Corporate Archivist, Corning Glass Works, Corning, New York; Hazel Confair, United Methodist Homes, Lewisburg, Pennsylvania; Clair Conway, Schwenkfelder Library, Pennsburg, Pennsylvania; Samuel Dornsife, Williamsport, Pennsylvania; Roman M. Dubenko, Ukranian Heritage Studies Center, Jenkintown, Pennsylvania; Gail Getz, William Penn Memorial Museum, Harrisburg, Pennsylvania; Charles Gladfelter, Adams County Historical Society, Gettysburg, Pennsylvania; Ruth K. Hagy, Chester County Historical

Society, West Chester, Pennsylvania; Jean W. Haines, McClure, Pennsylvania; Lois L. Hoerstkaamp, Gasconade County Historical Society, Hermann, Missouri; Christine M. Izack, Ukrainian Heritage Studies Center, Jenkintown, Pennsylvania; Allen Keyser, East Greenville, Pennsylvania; Carol Light, Lebanon County Historical Society, Lebanon, Pennsylvania; Mamelok Press Ltd., Suffolk, England; Salinda Matt, Lancaster Historical Society, Lancaster, Pennsylvania; Viola Miller, Lenhartsville, Pennsylvania; Historical Society of Montgomery County, Norristown, Pennsylvania; Gladys Murray, Centre County Historical Society, Bellefonte, Pennsylvania; William T. Parsons Pennsylvania Folklife, Collegeville, Pennsylvania; Historical Society of Perry County, New Bloomfield, Pennsylvania; Theodore Reed, The Reading Public Museum and Art Gallery, Reading, Pennsylvania; Jack D. Rimer, Pittsburgh, Pennsylvania; Edith Robinson, United Methodist Homes, Lewisburg, Pennsylvania; Malcolm A. Rogers, Riverhead, New York; Joan L. Romig, Historical Society of Dauphin County, Harrisburg, Pennsylvania; Geno Sartori, Brandon Memorabilia, New York; Marilyn Schopfer, C. A. Reed, Williamsport, Pennsylvania; Madeline Selfridge, Norco, California; Anna M. Sero, National Museum of American History, Washington, D. C.; Eugene E. Smith, Philadelphia, Pennsylvania; Phillip V. Snyder, New York; Janet Shadel Spillman, Curator, American Glass, Corning Museum of Glass, Corning, New York; Lenore Swoiskin, Archivist, Sears, Roebuck and Company, Chicago, Illinois; Neville Thompson, The Henry Francis du Pont Winterthur Museum, Winterthur, Delaware; Pat Tomes, The Historical Society of York County, York, Pennsylvania; Laura Walter, Mifflinburg, Pennsylvania; Marion Watts, Saint Genevieve, Missouri; Gail Winkler, The Atheneum, Philadelphia, Pennsylvania; Harold E. Yoder, Jr., The Historical Society of Berks County, Reading, Pennsylvania; Sister Virginia Zapotocky, Harrisburg, Pennsylvania.

Contemporary Pennsylvania craftspersons willing to demonstrate scratch-carving of eggs:
Evelyn Althouse/35 Queen Street/Ephrata 17522
Marie Foust/1004 Main Street/Watsontown 17777
Nada Gray/715 Market Street/Lewisburg 17837
Joan Maurer/303 Vine Street/New Berlin 17855
Annie Morgalis/300 Pine Hill/Minersville 17954
Marilyn Mosheim/Box 87 RD/Zionville 18092
Karen Rozell/404 Bloom Street/Danville 17821

## Public Collections of Christmas Ornaments

Chester County Historical Society
225 North High Street/West Chester, PA 19380

Victorian tree in December featuring glass ornaments as well as paper; outstanding collection of cotton-covered cardboard, handmade Dresdens tinsel and scraps.

Lycoming County Historical Society
848 West Fourth Street/Williamsport, PA 17701

Victorian tree in December with antique tinsel and scrap ornaments

Oral Traditions Project
Union County Historical Society
Courthouse/Second and Saint Louis Streets
Lewisburg, PA 17837

Ornament exhibit in December and January featuring flat cardboard, glass, tinsel and scrap. paper dolls—originals and reproductions as well as ornament classes

Pennsylvania Farm Museum
2451 Kissel Hill Road/Lancaster, PA 17601

Twelve-foot Victorian tree decorated in December with handmade items, antique ornaments, and memorabilia of the 19th century; accompanying toy exhibit in Gallery, Visitor Center; annual celebration of Christmas at Landis Valley

Pennsylvania Historical and Museum Commission
William Penn Memorial Museum
Third and North Streets/Harrisburg, PA 17120

Outstanding collection of kugels, flat paper, Dresdens, as well as scrap and tinsel ornaments, rarely on display—arrangements must be made in advance with the curator

Slifer House Museum
Lewisburg United Methodist Homes
Lewisburg, PA 17837

1862 mansion designed by Samuel Sloan decorated for the holidays in December; Victorian evening soiree first Saturday—reservations required; Open House; tours by appointment

The Historical Society of York County
Horace Bonham House/152 East Market Street
York, PA 17403

Victorian house decorated in December with tree and antique ornaments; tours by appointment

## Public Collections of Eggs

The Historical Society of Berks County
940 Centre Avenue/Reading, PA 19601

Varied collection of scratched and wax-resist eggs

Goschenhoppen Historians, Inc.
Box 576/Greenlane, PA 18054

Binsa-graws, scratched, wax-resist eggs

Heritage Center of Lancaster County
Center Square/Lancaster, PA 17604

Scratched eggs

Lancaster County Historical Society
230 North President Ave./Lancaster, PA 17603

Scratched and painted eggs

Lititz Historical Foundation
137-139 East Main Street/Lititz, PA 17543

Scratched eggs

The Historical Society of Montgomery County
1654 DeKalb/Norristown, PA 19401

One scratched egg

Our Lady of Czestochowa/Doylestown, PA 18901

Wax-resist eggs

Pennsylvania Folklife Collection
Box 92/Collegeville, PA 19426

Scratched and wax-resist eggs

Pennsylvania Hist. Museum Commission
William Penn Memorial Museum
3rd and North Streets/Harrisburg, PA 17120

Wax-resist eggs

Philadelphia Museum of Art
Benjamin Franklin Pkwy/Philadelphia, PA 19101

Scratched and wax-resist eggs

Schwenkfelder Library/Pennsburg, PA 18073

Scratched eggs

The Historical Society of York County
250 East Market Street/York, PA 17403

Scratched and wax-resist eggs

Arrangements should be made in advance with the curators of these museums to study the egg collections for they are on permanent display only at the Philadelphia Museum of Art and the Historical Society of Montgomery County.

## Sources of Supplies

Beistle Company
Box 10/Shippensburg, PA 17257

Honeycombed tissue paper and decorations for holidays

Brandon Memorabilia
222 East 51st Street/New York, NY 10022

Reproduction scraps and gold paper items

Hanusey Music and Gifts
344 W. Girard Avenue/Philadelphia, PA 19123

Directions, dyes, and tools for pysanka

Hobby House Press
900 Frederick Street/Cumberland, MD 21502

Kits for heads and bodies of paper dolls by Elsbeth

Hoffman's Hatchery/Gratz, PA 17030

Blown eggs

The Stephen Lawrence Co.
S. Hackensack, NJ 07606

Glazed paper

Lyco Merchandise
1016 Memorial Drive/Williamsport, PA 17701

Decoupage, flowers, and gold paper trim

Mel-Co Printing Company
255 Market Street/Sunbury, PA 17801

Paper and patterns for folded stars

Neece Paper Company
1307 Hadtner Street/Williamsport, PA 17701

Reproduction glass ornaments, Victorian wrapping paper, and books (October-January only)

Our Nest Egg
205 S. 5th Street/Mapleton, Iowa 51034

Blown eggs and egg stands

Madelaine Selfridge
P. O. Box 413/Norco, CA 91760

Antique paper dolls and scraps

Schlitz Goose Farm
Box P. C./Bancroft, Iowa 50517

Blown eggs and egg stands

Surma
11 East 7th Street/New York, NY 10003

Directions, dyes and tools for pysanka

Tall-Fox Novelty Company
440 Broad Street/Montoursville, PA 17754

Crepe paper and craft supplies

Ukranian Gift Shop
2422 Central Avenue, N. E.
Minneapolis, Minn. 55418

Directions, dyes and tools for pysanka

Westvaco Corporation
C. A. Reed Division
Routes 11 and 15/Shamokin Dam, PA 17876
416 West 3rd Street/Williamsport, PA 17701

Crepe paper and doilies